WHAT IT TAKES TO CREATE
WINNING PRESENTATIONS

The art of
strategic storytelling

———

What it takes to create

WINNING
PRESENTATIONS

Why being a good presenter is
often not enough and why the
best ideas don't always win

DAVID FISH

First published in 2023 by No Two Fish Pty Ltd

A catalogue entry for this book is available from the National Library of Australia.

ISBN: 978-1-923007-0-55

Printed in Australia by McPherson's Printing
Book production and text design by Publish Central
Cover design by Pipeline Design

The paper this book is printed on is certified as environmentally friendly.

CONTENTS

INTRODUCTION

THE PITCH WE HAD TO WIN

I was Head of Strategy at a London ad agency when BMW approached us to pitch; we didn't have a car client at the agency, and the CEO wanted one. Car clients look good on your credentials, and often lead to interesting and creative work. And they tend to pay well.

This was a big deal, so there was a lot of pressure.

Everyone in the company had a point of view on the pitch and the presentation. Feedback, ideas and slides came from everywhere, every day, right up to the moment we signed in at the reception deck. Even the cleaner had contributed.

The deck grew more enormous and more unwieldy as sections grew, and ideas merged and morphed. Keeping control of this beast was challenging. The laptop complained about saving such a large file. You know you are headed for trouble when there is time for a coffee while the icon spins and the hard drive whirs.

At the core of this troubled presentation was a major issue – we had lost sight of the problem we were trying to solve for the client. In fact, I'm not sure we ever fully understood this. As a result, the work was quickly becoming all about us. Not the potential client – *us*. How wonderfully creative we were, how smart we were (that was my – quite long – section), how much we loved cars (especially BMWs) and how fantastic our process was.

Did we mention how good we were?

With five presenters – yes, *five*, including the company CEO – and over 100 amazing slides (the creative team had excelled in design, videos and animations), we barely mentioned anything that resembled what *they* wanted, let alone getting down into what they might need from us. Acronyms flowed as we ploughed through the slides, each presenter taking longer than rehearsed as they embellished already irrelevant stories for the increasingly bored client.

It became a show about how in love we were with our slides and our ideas. It felt like, at certain moments, we might stop the presentation to slap each other on the back, revelling in how great this deck was and how well we were presenting.

As we powered on obliviously, the clients – a line of them all suited and wearing ties, sitting opposite us across the table – were not sharing our enthusiasm. They fluctuated between agitation, boredom, fear, bewilderment and, at times, outright visible confusion. You know, the face when your pet turns its head to the side as if to say, 'I have no idea what you want from me'. That is what we were facing. But with no other choice, we continued.

How did we get from the Scissor Sisters (an early 2000s pop band) squashed in a Mini with a glitter ball to a BMW motorbike surfing off the coast of Cornwall? Honestly, I wasn't even sure at that moment, and I wrote the damn presentation. We were so far off course after 30 minutes that as the next 60 ticked by, it started to become painful for us all. We would have been better off packing it in and going for a beer.

As we were shown out by a relieved client and into a very clinical white reception area, where our competitors were waiting, all suited up, our CEO turned and high-fived everyone on the team and yelled out, 'F***ing way to go, team, smashed it!' The startled receptionist reached for the security button, and our competitors were left wondering.

They had nothing to worry about.

This was the cherry on a very soggy cake. We went along with him, but we were all confused. Was he at the same pitch as us? Could he not sense the mood towards the end, that air of 'when will this finish'?

As he closed the door to his own BMW, he turned to me and the creative director, smiled and said, 'We'll never hear from them again.' A quick squeak of the tyres and BMW was behind us.

He was right. We never received a call to 'officially' tell us we didn't win.

And we didn't need one.

EPIPHANY: PRESENTATION SKILLS ALONE ARE NOT ENOUGH

The debrief for this calamity, however, was one of my career's most productive, constructive and enlightening. We diligently went through each stage, not to find blame (if we wanted to fire those responsible, there wouldn't be anybody left in the agency) but to extract learnings, lessons and clear action points. We saw this as the best training ground for eventually winning a car client and, within a couple of months, that was the case. When Hyundai briefed us on the launch of the i30, we nailed it: not just a car client but a new car launch for an emerging brand with substantial budgets.

Although we later came out on top, the BMW presentation was a painful experience, and some 20-plus years on I can still vividly recall many details that I would rather not have burned into my memory. Losing is a painful experience, and if you are a competitive person or in any kind of sales role, you are not taking part to come second or for the participation award. Whoever said 'it's taking part that matters' wasn't in sales.

I was both frustrated and intrigued when we lost, which motivated me to try to better understand what it takes to be a great presenter. But as I learned more about the nuances of pitching strategies, ideas, solutions and content that you need others to take forward on your behalf, this became what it takes to consistently create a *winning* presentation, a change I had not predicted when I embarked on this work.

I can't tell you how many presentations I have created, curated or sat through and wished I didn't have to endure or ever see again. But it's a lot. A *lot*. With that BMW pitch near the top of the list.

After nearly 30 years of working worldwide in marketing, advertising and media strategy roles, I have seen it all. The outlandishly big ideas, the brand launches and re-launches, the new technology platforms, tender responses, campaign summaries, agency pitches and countless hundreds of media presentations covering every channel you can imagine and a few obscure ones too.

At the heart of all these presentations is a need to get an audience to buy into a strategy, idea or solution by taking them on a journey that connects what you know to what they need. This audience is seeing this content for the first time. So it needs to be delivered in such a way that they can understand it, buy into it, convince others of its benefits and, ultimately, give you the outcome you desire: approve the strategy, buy the idea or sign off on the solution. That is what it means to deliver a presentation that wins over the audience and wins the business over the competition.

The lessons from losing

I, like so many I now work with, had put a lot of effort into my presentation skills and a lot less time into thinking about the actual structure of my presentation's content beyond making it look amazing. As I studied the various presentations I was creating, reviewing and subjected to sitting through, it became evident very quickly that a lot of training is geared towards the keynote end of the market: how to deliver grandiose presentations that leave a lasting impression. But very little focus is placed on creating presentations that support the selling of ideas or strategic solutions that give the sales and strategy professionals direction on how to build something with utility for them and the audience.

These are not presentations created over several months and rehearsed to be delivered repeatedly on grand stages. No, these are presentations created in weeks, days and hours and delivered once, on big screens and small, in coffee shops and via online meetings. They are delivered once to an audience who, after seeing the presentation for the first time, have to recall the key points, find the slides they need, and then deliver your idea to the next person and possibly the next.

The critical difference between what I and many others learned as a presenter and what is needed when selling ideas is that these presentations have to connect the audience to the content so that the audience can become the presenter after just one viewing. And they have to be built to support not just you in presenting with confidence, something that you may only have just put the finishing touches to, but also what the audience needs when you leave. You need to help them review, cut down and re-share your content. This was the critical difference between what I had been focused on in developing my presenting skills and what I needed to work on to create winning presentations. From then on, everything in my approach changed. And so did my win rate.

> **Presentations have to connect the audience to the content so that the audience can become the presenter after just one viewing.**

In one of my earlier marketing roles as a brand manager in a technology firm, I was sent on a week-long spin selling course with our sales team. At the time, I didn't see the relevance of most of what I was learning. *I'm in marketing, what has selling got to do with me?* was my slightly arrogant thought process. This training was based on the work of Neil Rackham, the author of the classic sales methodology book, *Spin Selling*.

During the week there was this one story shared by the trainers that many in the room found challenging but now makes more sense to me than it did at the time. It was the story of a very experienced and successful sales manager who was asked how he had managed to secure a multimillion-dollar sale to a major oil company. What he had worked out was that when you move from selling simple solutions that someone can buy on the spot to bigger and more complex ideas, your role changes. In the bigger sales, you only play a small part in the selling. The real selling goes on when you're not there, after you leave, after you have presented and left them with your content. It is then that the people you sold to go back and try to convince others, and they do that with your content but without you there to present it. This sales manager stated he was certain that his success was because he spent a lot of time trying to make sure the people he talked to knew how to sell for him. He saw his role like the director of a play. He was there during rehearsals but he wasn't on stage during the performance – for that he could only watch and hope he had done enough for the message to land.

As my experience grew and I spent more time in the intersection of sales and marketing, I began to see the value of this particular course and was grateful I had the opportunity to learn such powerful sales skills. I began to enjoy measuring the impact of my work through the impact on sales. It was an important early lesson that has served me well ever since.

EVERYONE IS SELLING SOMETHING

Many in the media world, from strategists to media owners to agencies and even some within client organisations, don't think their role is to sell; some even see the concept of 'selling something' as beneath them or a little grubby. If you are presenting to get an outcome from the audience, you can call it, think of it or describe it however you like in whatever way makes you feel okay with life, but to me, this is selling. And it is a critical difference between a keynote, inspirational or information-style presentation and what this book deals with: presentations that help you *sell*.

And because in this business the sale is rarely instant or on the spot, I define the 'win' as what you need to happen as a result of this presentation to keep you in the game. How does this presentation give you what you need to connect your ideas to your audience? And how does it give them what they need to take this forward with the confidence to champion what you have shared? That is a win that keeps you in the game. Without this, your ideas are dead and the selling is over.

To win consistently, you have to understand what it takes to create presentations designed to sell your ideas.

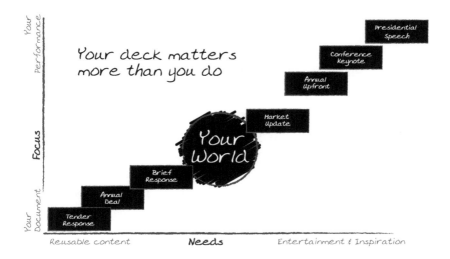

To win consistently, you have to understand what it takes to create presentations designed to sell your ideas in this way, and these, as I have learnt and will share with you, don't follow the conventional and corporate rules or approaches peddled by the mass-market training firms geared to a very different style and purpose of presentation. No, you need very specific and tailored tools to successfully sell your ideas.

AND SO, TO THE PRESENTATIONS THEMSELVES

Let's confront the underlying issue that the explosion of online meetings has dramatically highlighted. Most presentations are dull and overly long and, honestly, they are really quite awful at the job they need to do. As a result, very few people are excited by the prospect of sitting through another hour-long carousel of slides.

And there are more internal meetings consuming both time and head space. Agencies have an increasing number of their own products to educate their teams and present their own internal updates on. There are more vendors vying for the attention of media buyers and clients who occasionally take the time to entertain a media owner's presentation.

When there is a moment to share your ideas, that moment is precious and shouldn't be wasted with a presentation that doesn't do your ideas justice or do anything to give the audience a reason to see you again.

Why am I here?

You probably know that feeling just a few minutes in when it becomes clear that nothing you are seeing is of interest, or it really isn't that clear what you are seeing or why you are there, or how you can use any of this content to support what you need. And now you would rather not be there, but you are trapped for the next 55 minutes unless someone pulls the fire alarm and saves you, or you can fake an important text message that gives you a reason to leave. (Yes, that really does happen, more than you might realise.)

Slide after slide flies across the screen, often more than can be comfortably presented and certainly more than is needed, with the presenter maintaining a healthy jog to try to get through them. The slides are jam-packed, too, overflowing with information, possibly from a misguided attempt to cut down the number of slides by adding more to each slide. The jargon flows in a presentation built around what the presenter wants to share, what they want to tell the world about them and how great they are, but even they stumble and struggle to explain certain slides or fail to cover every point the slide appears to make.

At times it is clear that this isn't one presentation but a collective effort where the joins are obvious as sections clunk together or take a completely new direction as the next person steps up to tell you what they need you to know about how great their products are too, even though it's obvious with what you have already seen so far.

It is clear there has been very little thought given to the person on the receiving end and even less thought to how the content is put together to engage the audience. Sections come and go with no link, connection or flow; I mean, beyond good-looking stock images and the odd cat picture, they do little to draw in the audience or give them a reason to be there, let alone stay for the full hour or be engaged and moved to action. And some presentations should simply not exist at all; they serve no purpose other than to push information out into the world, often information the world didn't ask for or need.

Dale Carnegie makes his view on this very clear in his classic book on interpersonal persuasion, *How to Win Friends and Influence People*: 'You are interested in what you want...the rest of us are just like you: we are interested in what we want. So the only way on earth to influence other people is to talk about what they want and show them how to get it.'

Surely we can do better than this?

Now that's the rant, but here is the underlying issue. *This isn't working.* There is great thinking, amazing ideas and incredible solutions to real problems that deserve better.

You probably work in an organisation with products or services of great value to others; otherwise, why would you work there, and why would this organisation exist? You probably have brilliant minds around you, people who inspire you with what they can come up with, and you are excited to share this with the world, convinced you have something of real value to share. And yet, others don't always see what you see or get as excited as you are. They don't always call you back or take your ideas forward. You don't always win.

Days, weeks and months of work are being lost on audiences who can't keep up and sometimes have no idea what is hitting them, what this all means to them or how they can take what they are seeing and share it with others to get their much-needed buy-in.

And yet you have been trained to present, to become a more articulate presenter. Why is this still happening?

Being a good presenter, even the best presenter, now often confined to a tiny window on a screen of faces, cannot save even an average presentation from crashing and burning, taking with it the great idea, possibly the best idea, maybe even a solution the client really needs but that is now lost in a sea of complexity and confusion.

The issue is not how well you present; it is what you present and why this matters to them, the audience, the people giving up their time to see your content and how they connect with your content and can take what you present and become an advocate for your ideas.

Nancy Duarte made this point beautifully in her book *Resonate*, referring to the need to make this connection: ' ... that connection is why average ideas sometimes get traction and brilliant ideas die – it all comes down to how the ideas are presented'.

The new testing ground

When I was in charge of strategy for a media sales company, I worked closely with the sales team to construct some of their more significant presentations. Unlike my previous agency and client marketing roles, this team produced a heck of a lot of presentations in all shapes and sizes every day, sometimes several a day. And all of them had one clear goal: to convince someone to buy what we had to sell. To win the business.

This took everything I had learnt and been testing in my presentations to another level. The sales and commercial impact were easy to measure, and subtle changes could be tested at scale quickly. I played with new ways to construct content, tell stories and help the account managers to deliver the message and the audience – the buyer of these ideas – take what we had presented and be able to sell our ideas to someone, using the story and specific slides we had carefully designed to help them do just that.

From process to tools

Since then, countless versions of my strategic process have been designed to aid the creation of more compelling content in more effective presentations for small teams through to global agency networks pitching for billion-dollar contracts.

Over time, my focus shifted from seeing this as a rigid process, a fixed set of steps that must be followed in strict order, to becoming a more flexible methodology that has now evolved into a set of tools that work independently, each solving a specific challenge, as well as working together to build greater depth and capability for those who want to become true presentation masters, to master the art of Strategic Storytelling.

Each stage of learning and refining has led to simplifying the application, broadening it, and increasing its effectiveness as measured through the impact of the training and coaching I now deliver and the feedback I get from those using these tools to achieve more successful and consistent delivery.

TIME FOR CHANGE

Whether you're a sales director, sales manager, account manager, strategist or client charged with presenting ideas you need someone else to connect with, buy into and take forward on your behalf, this book will take you on a journey to build your confidence as a presenter and to move you from being a Hopeful Presenter to a Strategic Storyteller.

And this is why it matters.

The problem I often hear people express when we start working together is that their presentation skills are letting them down; they feel like they could win more if they were better presenters. There is a thought bubble that they need to go to the 'Obama School of Presidential Speaker Training'.

But as we chat, what we learn is that the challenges they face have little to do with their skills on their feet and far more to do with what they are presenting. They can relate strongly to a combination of the following statements:

- ▶ I hope our ideas resonate with someone in the audience.
- ▶ I hope we have something they need.
- ▶ I hope they can see how we can solve a problem for them.
- ▶ I hope we don't overwhelm them with all of our content, acronyms and jargon.
- ▶ I hope they can see the bigger idea in all of the stuff we have.
- ▶ I hope they can find what they need to present our ideas.
- ▶ I hope they can follow along and we don't lose them.
- ▶ I hope I can land all the key points and not get lost in the slides.
- ▶ I hope we don't spend too much time just talking about us.
- ▶ I hope they can remember what this is all about when they come back to review our content in a few days.
- ▶ I hope I can explain why this matters when I get asked what this is all about.
- ▶ I hope I don't need to provide a summary slide, as I have no idea where to start.

They are what I call a 'Hopeful Presenter'. And hope has never been a great sales or presentation strategy in my experience.

As these challenges remain unresolved, they slowly slip down the continuum of darkness. They start to get feedback from clients that they missed the brief and they feel a little baffled. Buyers are 'forgetting' them or the vital ideas at the critical point when they are making the decision.

Win rates fall.

They start to question other teams: the strategy team made it too complicated; the ideas team missed the insight and the ideas were too big. There is increasing tension internally; the producers of the great idea and the seller start blaming each other. The strategists start doing their own presentations, losing confidence in sales – 'They can't sell my ideas, so I'll do it.'

Confidence plummets, conversion rates fall further and, under pressure because they are not selling, they start to doubt themselves. If the spiral continues unchecked it can end up with a desperate seller.

Sound a bit dramatic? It's supposed to be, to get your attention on how bad things can get if this problem is left unchecked or mis-diagnosed, and it's why this book and the change that I see as being possible matters to you.

How many of those 'hope' statements resonated with you? They come from listening to those I train and coach and in research conducted for this book, and they have defined the challenges a Hopeful Presenter faces perfectly.

And this is that change, the change I see as being possible from this place of hope to being a confident Strategic Storyteller.

In all my years obsessing about this topic, two things have remained timeless that this book addresses head on:

▶ Too many presentations are self-serving and full of internal jargon with badly organised content rendering them complex, confusing and missing what the audience needs to see, so much so that even the most accomplished and polished speaker can't save them from losing the audience on the day.

▶ Great ideas, fabulous ideas, the best strategy, and even the right approach for a client can all easily get lost in the sea of slides in presentations that don't connect the audience to the content and enable them to take your ideas forward.

When you are just the first presentation of the many required to get your ideas across the line, these two challenges alone will severely limit your success.

HOW TO USE THIS BOOK

This practical how-to book teaches how to overcome these and other core challenges that stop presentations from winning. It can be used to help refresh this knowledge every time you develop a new presentation on its own, and alongside the training and coaching I deliver on this topic.

In part I, I expand on the context and the unique challenges faced daily by those creating presentations that need to land an idea, get buy-in to a strategy or are charged with selling ideas. Challenges that may need to be better understood to be resolved.

In my experience, it is sadly very rare for clients – the recipients of these presentations – to provide frank and directional feedback, which means it is hard to know how they felt when you presented, what they thought about how you structured and delivered your content and why you didn't get a call back or any follow up and why you didn't win. This first part will change that.

In part II, I unpack the 12 tools, which are organised into the four toolboxes that guide creating presentations. These are:

- ▶ **Clear** about why this presentation exists, who it is for and what matters to them.
- ▶ **Concise** in the organisation and visualisation of the content and being able to turn *every* presentation into a single page.
- ▶ **Compelling** through the story that is told to bring the audience into your content and connect them emotionally to what you have to offer.
- ▶ **Simple**, which is the ultimate goal for a Strategic Storyteller who wants to be armed with the highest-level view of their work, prepared to share this with anyone in any situation while ensuring others are able to take their ideas forward, even if they never see a slide.

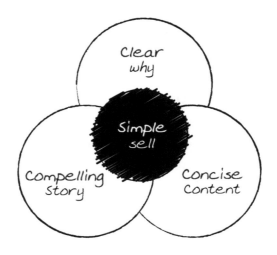

From Hopeful Presenter to Strategic Storyteller

These tools can be used individually to raise the bar on a specific skill or area of challenge within the development process or as a set of tools supporting the end-to-end development and delivery of the presentation.

I suggest you read the book through once and then decide which sections of part II are most relevant to you and go back over these, taking the time to apply the exercises as you develop your next presentation or review a current one.

NOBODY LIKES LOSING

My aim with this book, and the training and coaching that sits around it, is that you never have to experience massive presentation failure and make all of the mistakes I made in my early career, and have since gone on to see repeated time and time again. I want to help you avoid that losing feeling. Our BMW presentation, of course, wasn't my only loss, but it was a significant one. These losses and many more wins equate to several hundreds of millions of dollars of sales pitches and wins. From creating, presenting, reviewing and sitting through presentations as the client, I have gathered learnings from seeing tens of thousands of slides. Over the years, these have become tips for strategists, clients and account managers; they then became tools that are easy to learn, practical and highly effective, and now they form the core of this book.

This book will equip you to create clear, concise, compelling and simple presentations, something I wish I had when we pitched for BMW. We probably would have won because we certainly had the best ideas.

Ultimately, I want you to avoid that sinking feeling when you can see the audience is no longer with you; your great ideas are getting lost in a bad presentation that even you, one of the best presenters, can't save.

Even when you have the best idea, the presentation of that idea can make or break it, and when you don't have the best idea, the packaging of the concept within a well-constructed sales presentation can elevate it to a winner.

Imagine having the best idea in a well-constructed presentation; it's *definitely* a winner.

Part I

WHY THE BEST IDEAS DON'T ALWAYS WIN

CHALLENGES THAT UNDERMINE GREAT IDEAS

Clients don't generally tell you that you bored the pants off them talking about yourself for over an hour, that they didn't understand most of what you presented or couldn't figure out how to make it work for them, or that they were lost after the first 10 minutes and started to write out their to-do list for the week while making it look like they were taking notes.

FIGURING OUT WHY YOUR PRESENTATION WENT WRONG

I often hear people say they don't really know why they didn't win, or they blame something completely unconnected to the actual reason. Internally this becomes 'our idea was not good enough' or 'we missed the brief'. A witch hunt takes place looking for someone to blame when the real cause will probably never be found through your eyes; only the audience knows where it all went wrong.

I will now share the most common challenges that can derail you and stop your presentations from being an effective sales tool that should help you win.

Something for everyone

Have you ever sat through a presentation or even read a book and thought, *This isn't for me, what is this all about?* or *Why am I bothering with this?* That isn't how you want your audience to feel when you present, but I can't tell how often this happens.

This usually occurs when the audience for this specific presentation isn't clearly identified upfront. As a result, different pieces of content get added for everyone 'who might be interested' or who might attend the meeting. All bases get covered. What could have been a clear message for the right audience, addressing a clear problem, becomes a waffly rambling collection of something for everyone.

The hope that *something* sticks, that there is something in this that someone might get excited about, is not a great place to start.

Presentations without an anchor

When you start without a clear idea of who your audience is, what problem they have or what their underlying needs are, you are like a boat in a harbour without an anchor, at risk of drifting off at any moment. And drift you will as the opinions, content and ideas of others creep in during the building of your presentation, because you were not focused enough at the outset.

To take the audience on your journey showing how you solve their problem you don't just need to know what the high-level problem is; you need to understand what it means to them, what the impact is of having this problem and what could be at stake if it isn't solved. This fundamental understanding is core not just to how your presentation can be crafted around a compelling story; it is core to how every story brings a reader in. But this understanding does more than provide a nice way into your story. It is critical to how you establish the value in your ideas for your audience and how you curate the content to make this clear to them.

Solving a specific problem with a narrative aimed at the audience who cares about this being solved ensures your message cuts through with the people who matter, those for whom you deliver real value.

Bland and generic messages

Ryanair is a low-cost airline based out of Ireland, but according to aviation specialist Cirium, which provides analytics and data on air travel, Ryanair Holdings is the world's fifth biggest carrier, Europe's biggest airline and the largest in the world outside the US (home to the top four carriers: American Airlines, Delta Air Lines, United Airlines and Southwest Airlines).

Since their inception in 1984 with 25 employees and one aircraft, Ryanair have been clear on one thing – who their audience is, and that is the fare-conscious customer. Those who otherwise would have chosen an alternative mode of transportation or not travelled at all.

They have never tried to be anything more to anyone other than the budget-conscious traveller who wants a no-frills service. There have been no attempts at business class or upmarket service offerings. If you want frills, don't fly with Ryanair is clearly the message, and this has played out in everything from advertising to the often controversial comments from the airline CEO, Michael O'Leary, which include this infamous line: 'Are we going to say sorry for our lack of customer service? Absolutely not.' This is all reinforcing that you get what you pay for – and with Ryanair, you are not paying very much.

Now, you might be thinking, *Doesn't this put some people off? Don't they alienate people with comments like this?* And the answer is yes, and that is why it works. This leads to very clear messaging and very direct points that alienate many but attract those who matter most to them: the audience they are targeting who values what they provide. It is a win–win, to the point of winning against established airlines such as British Airways as well as other low-cost carriers such as EasyJet. Knowing your audience means you can speak to them and their specific needs.

While Ryanair's approach may be extreme, I have sadly worked with many clients who miss this point in marketing and waste millions on bland and generic messages in advertising aimed at everyone but targeting no-one, ads that fail to have an impact because no-one cares. And I see this every day in presentations as well, with the same effect.

Know your audience and focus everything on them. This should be a core principle for the design of every presentation.

Generic messaging leads to expansion

When you are not clear about whom you are creating content for, you become generic in your points; you solve general problems with broad and sweeping statements and, worse still, you add more and more content trying to cover not just one problem – where you can deliver real value – but every problem that might exist for those in the room. This is where your presentation becomes bloated with content, waffly, complex and hard to navigate for you and the audience, who are probably wondering why they are there, given so much seems to be aimed at someone other than them.

The more you add, the more you dilute the value of your core idea, which started by solving a specific problem and is now solving all of the world's problems in 90 slides. It becomes harder for the audience to hear your point, and to connect with what you are saying and the benefit to them. This, in turn, makes it harder for them to recall any of what was presented or to find that one useful piece now lost in a sea of content for everyone.

BUT WHO IS MY AUDIENCE?

Now, at this point, I am often asked what to do when you don't know who might attend your presentation; maybe you have a proactive idea (an idea you have developed yourself that you want to take to the world) or the group you present to invites lots of people but only a few ever show up, and you are never really sure who this will be until you walk into the room.

In these instances, you need to move from thinking about your audience as specific people – the names of those attending – to thinking about roles. What type of role within the group you are presenting to has the problem you are solving, and what roles can help carry your ideas forward? Roles exist even without people – vacant roles in organisations, for instance – and roles have characteristics you can determine without knowing who specifically holds that role.

When you think about *roles* and not *people*, you remove the barrier of who might attend and think instead about which roles might have the problem you can solve and, therefore, which roles your ideas matter to.

Then think about what roles would be best placed to take what you present and convey it to others to get their buy-in.

Finally, what roles have influence over how your presentation is viewed – a subject matter expert or a role that controls the budget allocation?

Understanding these issues will enable you to make a call on which roles might attend. You might not know who, but you can view the roles likely to want to be across what you have and the roles you need there to make this a worthwhile exercise for you.

There are two important points here:

▸ If there is no-one present who could be the connector of your content to others, no role that has the ability to take your ideas forward, your presentation is unlikely to lead to anything positive and is probably going to be a waste of your time and theirs. Rescheduling when you can present to the right audience would be a better option for everybody.

▸ A presentation without a problem to solve is a presentation without a purpose. This means that without clearly defining the problem, you are wandering off into generic territory. You are essentially presenting your ideas and hoping to find a problem they might solve, and if you don't, your ideas will have no value.

Even if you don't have access to the client to undertake a detailed discovery with them before you present or you often pitch proactive ideas, you can still work out what problem you should be solving.

You might have to come up a level from a specific role within a client to look at this from a category perspective. At this level, there will be trade press articles, LinkedIn posts and rants, and a whole world of points of view on problems that companies in that sector are facing. Thinking about which of these your ideas can help solve will give you a good starting point.

By working through the audience in this way, you can move from not knowing who will attend and feeling paralysed about who your audience is to knowing the roles you want your content to resonate with.

THE CONTENT AVALANCHE

There will nearly always be more content than is needed, but how do you know what should stay and what should get left out?

I am very fortunate to have been exposed to this early in my career and have worked on what I call 'all sides of the fence' – in roles selling big ideas, strategic solutions and concepts as the strategic lead, and as the client briefing, reviewing and buying these strategies and ideas, as well as within media organisations that survive through the creation of content, audiences and technology solutions and the ability to com-mercialise this with advertisers' dollars. Each has given me a different perspective on how content comes together and how it needs to flow into a well-contained and concise structure, as well as what is desired and what is needed on the receiving end of this content.

> **There will nearly always be more content than is needed, but how do you know what should stay and what should get left out?**

It all started so well

All of your organisation's great resources worked hard to develop something compelling. Or you know you have a solid product and are keen to get this out into the world. In both cases, there is the genesis for a slide deck that should surely convert.

It just keeps coming

Everyone makes what seems like a valid argument for including their suggested content, but you can see there are competing priorities, and then one more 'new section to drop into the deck' lands in your inbox.

As the presentation continues to expand, even you are unsure of the point you are trying to land. Slides have come from several differ-ent teams: sales priorities, background slides, case studies, research, strategy, process and even team overview and legal slides. Somewhere in there is the solution and the answer to the audience's problem – if they can find it.

Always more than you need

When you can't control what goes in and what gets left out, it can become incredibly challenging, even frustrating, as you try to stay on top of all the content. When you leave too much in, you dilute your overall message; you can get lost and find it hard to present. The presentation can become hard to follow and confusing for the audience, making it difficult for them to determine whether they should care about specific pieces of information and what is truly important.

How do you say no to well-meaning contributors when everyone has a seemingly compelling reason for their content going in? How can you challenge senior stakeholders who 'know what this needs to be successful' and insist on the same company background and 'about us' slides going in every time?

Without becoming very clear upfront about what this presentation is there to do and the journey you want to take the audience on, defined by key points that form a flowing narrative from problem to resolution, wrestling content into an orderly structure will be incredibly challenging.

The view from the other side

It wasn't until I sat on the other side of the table – being presented to, desperately trying to find the bits of information I needed to take from this fire hose of information coming at me – that I really understood this challenge in all its glory.

As you create a presentation, you become intimately familiar with its content. You see it build. You add the sections and marvel over the incredible image you found. To you, it all makes sense, and that was precisely how I felt every time I built my presentations; I knew every slide, I knew what came next, I knew the point I was making, and I even smiled when an image I was super proud of finding came on screen.

I was a presentation genius.

Or so I thought.

The early indicators were the random audience questions about points I thought I had landed. Didn't you see slide seven with the cat and the baby (great image) under the heading 'We care'? Or the animation on slide 53 that clearly answered that question? Then the requests would come in for follow-up information, or for us to send over a revised section with particular information that was clear (I thought) in the presentation.

Or – worse – there were no questions at all, just silence.

The fire hose

When I became the client on the receiving end of many more presentations, it became clear what this was all about. I had confused my audiences with too much content that wasn't structured to keep them following along, and to compound things, this made it harder for them to find what they needed after the presentation.

As a client, you are seeing most (or all) of this information for the first time, and you don't know what is coming next or how things connect if it isn't made clear. As more and more content comes at you, it becomes even harder to stay on top of all this new information and make sense of it. It can feel like you are drinking from a fire hose of content. This can be particularly challenging if this is an area you don't know well or spend much time on, and it isn't as familiar to you as it is to the presenter; now, you are drowning.

Inevitably, when there is more content than time allows, the presenter speeds up their delivery in a valiant attempt to deliver 90 slides in under 60 minutes, which just makes this situation worse.

The harder you look, the more lost you get

As a client, I have often felt lost, confused and even frustrated when I could see there was the genesis of a good idea being presented to me but I couldn't see how I could take these slides and present them to my team or how I could explain exactly what was presented further up into the company for buy-in or sign-off. One thing I can be certain of is that if someone is confused by what they have seen, they are sure as hell not going to try to explain it to their boss.

What about this month's sale focus?

Now you might be saying, 'Yes, but how can I challenge a sales director pushing us to include this month's sales focus even if I know it's not the right fit?' I hear you.

However, you both want the same thing: to win the business. And to do that you have to deliver something the audience wants, delivered so they can see the value in your ideas and solutions and they can present on easily. If you miss this, whether you have this month's sales focus included is largely irrelevant because you will not get a call back, let alone land the sale, unless luck is on your side – and I have never favoured that as a tremendous long-term sales strategy.

The challenge of managing content and filtering this all starts when you are not clear on the change you see as possible. This is a simple 'from–to' that defines the beginning and end of your story in which all of your content fits; that is, all of the content that is relevant in getting from the problem to your known resolution.

Without this, you have little basis for making an argument for leaving things out. As a result, almost everything can end up going in. That will never end well. In my experience, the more you cram into one presentation, the harder it becomes to sustain a flow and connection, the less it cuts through, and the more likely it becomes that you will confuse your audience and lose them in the avalanche of slides.

> **One thing I can be certain of is that if someone is confused by what they have seen, they are sure as hell not going to try to explain it to their boss.**

HOUSTON, WE HAVE A PROBLEM – WITH POWERPOINT

Would you believe me if I said that a poorly prepared presentation was a contributing factor to the Space Shuttle *Columbia* disaster in 2003? *Columbia* suffered a catastrophic explosion on re-entry to Earth's atmosphere, killing everybody on board.

When the shuttle launched, a piece of the insulating foam broke off from its external tank and struck the thermal protection tiles on the orbiter's left wing. Similar foam shedding had occurred during previous Space Shuttle launches, causing damage that ranged from minor to near-catastrophic, but some engineers suspected that the damage to *Columbia* was more serious. During a resulting review of the integrity of the heat shield and the risks of bringing the shuttle back to Earth, the NASA Debris Assessment Team presented its analysis in a formal briefing to the Mission Evaluation Room within NASA that relied on PowerPoint slides from Boeing, who had conducted the tests on the heat shield in the past.

During the investigation of the disaster, Dr Edward Tufte of Yale University, an expert in information design and a pioneer in the field of data visualisation, studied how the slides used by the Debris Assessment Team in their briefing to the Mission Evaluation Room misrepresented key information.

One slide contained critical information, test data and findings relating to the shuttle's ability to withstand this type of incident that, if properly understood by the audience, could have changed the outcome. Here are the four key issues Dr Tufte identified, as summarised in the Accident Investigation Report:

▸ The heading didn't land on the critical point of the slide; in fact, it was seen as misleading. If all someone read was the heading, they could believe there was little cause for concern. This was not what the rest of the information on the slide explained, but they concluded that because of the sheer amount of information presented on the one slide, many would just read the heading.

▸ The language and layout meant that as the information flowed up within NASA, key explanations and essential information were filtered out as the emphasis on what was critical was not passed on.

▸ The slide had six levels of information. However, the information hierarchy wasn't logical, and the most critical information didn't come first. In fact, the most important information was the last point on a slide that contained over 100 words. This point was: 'One estimate of the debris that struck *Columbia* was 640 times larger than the data used to calibrate the model on which engineers based their damage assessments.'

It was determined that had different decisions been made based on this presentation, there may have been a different outcome for *Columbia* and the seven astronauts. A contributing factor in the loss of the Space Shuttle was the information on the slides wasn't easy to understand, the key points didn't land, and it wasn't easy to present this information without key details getting lost.

If the poor structure of a presentation can contribute to an aerospace disaster, imagine what it could be doing to your chances of landing that strategic presentation.

What guides you?

Rank these statements based on the order in which they are true for you, with one being most true and four being least true, and see what this highlights in your approach to structuring your content.

What guides you when you work to refine your content and build your final presentation?

1. The change you see as possible from the problem to your known resolution.

2. How sections connect to take the audience on a clear journey from their problem to your resolution, keeping only the content that supports these points.

3. What others suggest should be included, whether it is solving the audience's specific problem or not.

4. Content and slides you already have that are easy to drop in, even if they aren't quite on point for this particular presentation.

If 1 and 2 are not your top two, keep reading.

As if I have the time for this!

I know that in some situations when building a presentation, you might not get to see all the content with the luxury of time on your side.

However, once you have learnt how to layer content by laddering up to the most important point to control the flow of information, you can organise your content very quickly. You will be able to arrange slides like a deck of cards. You can deal the ace and then the king and queen, only going further if there is a real need to unpack detail after this. You can easily filter out the extra and weaker content and the 'add-ons' that don't connect or aren't needed within each section.

SELLING THE INGREDIENTS, NOT THE DISH

When you are hungry and in a rush to get to a meeting and looking to grab some lunch on the go, what is of greater value and utility to you, a tasty and warm ham and cheese toasty or a loaf of bread, packet of ham, some cheese slices, a tub of spread and a sandwich press?

There is a place for ingredients, but when you are trying to sell a premium strategic solution this is not it.

Your organisation will be awash with things you could sell, a veritable market stall of ingredients that could be combined to create solutions that solve problems, creating greater utility that increases both the value and the ease with which someone can buy what you have created for them. Like the warm toasty that solves your hunger and gives you exactly what you need as you whizz by on your way to the meeting. But the toasty doesn't form itself; it is made by bringing ingredients together to package them into a new, more interesting and appealing item.

The market stall of stuff

When you don't do the work, when you don't bring together ingredients to form tasty dishes, when you don't combine elements to make them easier to understand, of greater value and utility and easier to buy, you are putting the market stall on display.

You are selling the stuff that goes into your ideas, the raw ingredients, which brings with it several issues for you and your audience.

Combining creates value

How much would you pay for eggs, flour and water versus some beautiful pancakes to go with your morning coffee?

The ingredients are never worth as much as the dish; your solutions are the same.

When you do the work to bring elements together, your effort to curate and create increases the value of your ideas; conversely, the more you unpack and expose each contributing element (ingredient), the easier you make it for your audience to buy the more minor elements and not the total solution.

You make it much easier for them to negotiate on each item, one by one, devaluing your overall solution bit by bit. Sometimes this happens so stealthily that you hardly notice until it's too late, and you have given away all your IP and creativity for much less than it's worth as a total solution.

Increasing utility and ease

When you present how everything works together to solve your audience's problem and help them move forward, you increase the utility of your offering and make it easier for them to buy from you.

The Hopeful Presenter lays out lots of little pieces for the audience to pick at, like a seagull picking at chips dropped on the ground. The hope is that as the audience picks away, they can find what *they* think they need to help them move forward. They can put the pieces together and solve their problem from the market stall of stuff on display. This is often led by a lack of understanding of the real problem to be solved, which results in putting more *stuff* out in the hope something might just be right and catch their eye.

Sadly, often this simply isn't the case. Instead, they look at everything on display and don't see any usefulness in any of it.

You have also left them with a shopping list of ingredients and no-one to make up something tasty for dinner tonight. They are busy, and when you have finished presenting, they move on to the next presentation or item on their to-do list.

You have made it hard to buy you, so they don't.

> When you present how everything works together to solve their problem and help them move forward, you increase the utility of your offering and make it easier for them to buy from you.

By showing how everything works together, you increase the usefulness of your total solution because your audience can now see what this does for them and how it does it for them, why they need all these pieces, and the utility of what you have created for them. And you have made it easier for them too. There is less effort on their part to make sense of everything and, therefore, you become easier to buy; that is a winning approach.

Too much choice can be demotivating

As Barry Schwartz outlines in his great book *The Paradox of Choice*, giving people too much choice can be demotivating. Schwartz found that when consumers were presented with a selection of 24 different jams, only 3% of shoppers purchased; however, when only six jams were on display, 30% purchased.

When you put more out in the hope that something sticks, the opposite can be true, and you get less than if you had limited choice. This is certainly my experience when it comes to how you package your ideas and solutions within presentations.

The fear of too little and too big

Now, some fears often bubble up when I talk about reducing the number of products or ideas that go into one presentation. These are the fear of not having enough and the fear of making an idea too big and so overwhelming the audience when they just might want one part of it.

These fears are the drivers that lead to excessive content and allowing ingredients to be put out on display, *just in case*. There is a discipline to controlling the flow of information as well as curating how many choices you give the audience so they feel they have a degree of control and influence but not so much that they are overwhelmed and paralysed by the volume of information, products and ideas on offer.

Once you have learned how to organise, optimise and visualise your content, you will experience the power of being able to customise the choice while having much more precise control over how far down into the detail you go at any moment during the presentation. It is a skill that, once learnt, you will wonder how you ever survived without it.

A market stall will never charge the same for the ingredients as the restaurant does for the main course made up of the same ingredients. Your job is to become the chef, bringing the ingredients together to create tasty and premium dishes your audiences see as relevant and valuable to them.

Think back over your last few presentations and the outcomes of these. How often did you get the bigger idea across the line, the total solution, versus a client picking away at your content and moving forward with just some of the elements of the solution?

Now have a look at those presentations and give yourself a score from 1 to 5 for each, against these criteria:

▶ You have brought elements together and shown how they work together (5) or You included lots of ideas and products that the audience could pick at (1).

▶ There is a logical flow to the unpacking of the ideas from concept down into detail (5), or Everything is on display all at once or in no particular order (1).

Based on your responses, how easy did you make it to buy the total solution you wanted to sell? Which means scoring 4 and above.

IT'S ALL ABOUT YOU

I do not doubt that, given the opportunity, there is a lot you could share about what you do, why it is excellent, maybe how you work to create these great ideas, that unique seven-step process. And then there are all your products, tools and techniques, many of which have been given funky or abstract names to make them sound cool, modern, exciting, unique or premium.

You probably have your own internal language, a derivative of the industry jargon but given your own special twist. It makes your version sound that little bit fancier, more complex and potentially more important.

The question is how much all of this matters, not to you and the team around you who live and breathe this day in and day out, but to your audience?

Why should someone outside your organisation care about any of this?

I often see sales presentations that are just a story about the organisation, about what they do and how they do it. 'Can I have an hour of your time to come and talk exclusively about me and how great our company is?' 'No,' would be my answer. How about you?

> **The question is how much all of this matters, not to you and the team around you who live and breathe this day in and day out, but to your audience?**

Balance offsets boredom

The point is there needs to be some balance. Even if you are asked to present pure credentials, a 'why you' presentation, there needs to be some consideration given to what each part of your story means to your audience, why they should care, what benefit they get from whatever point you are making, and how it helps them solve a problem or move forward.

Without this, you risk boring them with a presentation that does little to connect and is easily forgotten.

By way of a straightforward but far too common example for my liking, it is nice that you have offices in every part of the country and can present a pretty map with the number of people in each location. But how often has that slide been presented to a client with one office and doing business from that one location? What is the value to them of your multi-location offering and smattering of people around the country who this client will never work with? Unless they need a multi-office solution, unless they see value in your network of offices, you just wasted a slide and five minutes on something that is just about you.

Other common sections that can lead you into an 'all about me' moment are:

▶ the company history or timeline, companies that have merged, and when new products were acquired and added

- ▶ the strategic approach or steps to creating ideas
- ▶ product catalogues and overviews of everything you do
- ▶ market share, audiences sizes and audiences by location
- ▶ approach to collecting, sorting and storing data.

It is not always that these sections shouldn't be in your presentation, but without thinking about the 'so what?', which is the benefit of this to your audience, you risk losing the audience's attention and engagement, particularly if this is the majority of the content you have in the whole presentation.

I was chatting to a chief marketing officer about this book and this particular topic came up and, before I could finish, they jumped straight in to tell me about a recent pitch they had just run to find a new agency partner. In a very animated fashion, they went on to say: 'We could not believe it. It was all about them, some magic process we were supposed to believe nobody else had ever come up with, all their proprietary tools with names that made no sense, of which I think I can recall one but couldn't tell you what it does or why we need it. And then, they finished off with why they thought they were amazing. They appeared to be oblivious to the fact that there was literally nothing in their 60-odd slides that gave us any reason to give a sh*t. They left thinking they did an amazing job, buzzing and probably slapping each other on the back, and will have no idea why they will never hear from us again.'

Sadly, in my experience this is not a one-off example but a common problem for both agencies and media sellers who spend way too much time just presenting 'about us' slides with no consideration to the 'so what?' for the audience.

The what and the why

You are probably thinking, *Hang on a minute here, surely they need to know who we are, what we do, how we do it and what makes us different, brilliant and amazing?*

Absolutely, they do.

Balance is about all these things in combination with the 'so what?' for them. When you can marry what you do with why that's a benefit to the audience, when you can describe how you do something along with what this enables or delivers for them, when who you are is aligned with what they value, then you can craft a narrative that will have meaning and depth to this specific audience. That is when your presentation has balance.

The other extreme is also to be avoided – just landing a stream of benefits for them with no substance behind what or how you deliver these amazing outcomes. A string of slides that promises to 'engage your audience, with transparency, in real time, maximising your first-party data, driving conversion, maximising profit and top-line growth' can become a game of buzzword bingo. This can feel shallow, lacking the substance and validation needed to give your audience confidence in your ability to deliver.

This can create dissonance between what you say and what they believe is possible based on what they see. They can become challenged by how amazing you are at hitting all the hot topics, but unclear exactly how you do it and, indeed, if you can.

Balance is about why the audience should care about your point, what this does for them and how you do it. When this works in harmony, you will avoid boring your audience or leaving them wondering.

CHECK YOUR BALANCE

Take a moment to go through one of your more detailed presentations – something, say, over 20 slides.

► How many of these slides describe how you came up with the work or what you do, your products and services? (about you)

► How many describe what the work does and the benefit or value it delivers to the audience? (about them)

► How many of your slide headings are named after or include references to your approach, or the name of your tools, products or the things you want to sell? (about you)

► How many slide headings give the audience a reason to care about what is on that slide and what it means to them? (about them)

► Where is your balance right now?

Everything can have value

I know many organisations have a fixed set of 'about us' slides or something similar they insist are included in every presentation.

While it would be clear I am not a fan of this generic approach, let us work with what we have. If you are faced with having to include a certain set of slides in every presentation, after each generic section create a specific slide that summarises the 'so what?'.

This new slide should make the connection between what you have just presented and what this delivers for the audience. Don't assume they will make this connection or that it is obvious or it doesn't matter; what you think is obvious is often completely missed by your audience, and you don't want to have long stretches of content that has no meaning for the audience if you want to keep them engaged.

THE LAST-HOPE TAXI RIDE

PowerPoint is reluctant to open; there are so many slides. You know you cannot get through them in the time you have, and with one tech hiccup you are done for. It's unclear where you can summarise because the slides jump from point to point and don't have clean sections to make edits easier.

Safely away from prying eyes, it's time for one last attempt to create some order in the taxi ride to the meeting. The appendix looks like a good place to dump slides that should never have made it this far. It is one last-ditch effort to create some semblance of a flow, to join things together. One more set of traffic lights and this might be possible.

That growing sense of dread

You know what you have still isn't what you want to present. It's long, doesn't flow as well as you would like, feels clunky to you and you know most of the content, and still, you are not as confident as you could be in remembering all of the critical points.

It isn't clear from the navigation what is coming next. The slide headings aren't that helpful at reminding you what each slide is about, let alone guiding the audience and helping them keep up with you and find the key points in your narrative. And there are slides that even you are not sure what the point of them is, and it's too late to get rid of them now.

How many times in the last few months have you found yourself franticly trying to organise slides in the final few moments before you have to present?

How many times have you created an appendix just to 'store slides' you don't have anywhere else for?

How often do you walk into a meeting knowing what you have is not the best story you could tell, or knowing there is no story at all but you have run out of time to make any more changes?

Sometimes the last few hours before you present is the first time you see everything together. While not ideal, I get that this happens and is often out of your control because you rely on other teams for content and to deliver slides for you to collate into a final deck.

Imagine if there was a way to quickly organise content, define a narrative and connect each section. That would surely help in such situations, as well as when you have more time to work through this properly, wouldn't it?

The missing link is knowing how to structure your content into a story, a story that has predefined sections with clear navigation through a flowing narrative. And the good news is there is only one structure you need to learn that will guide every presentation. Once you have mastered this, even in the last few hours you can quickly make a call on how to edit and move content. You will be able to look at each part of the deck and decide if it could be shorter to make the point you need to make. You will know how to work on sections rather than looking at the whole deck and being overwhelmed by just how much content you have and not knowing where to begin, with the pressure of the clock ticking down.

THE GREATEST SHOW WILL NEVER BE ENOUGH

You have made it to the meeting, the deck you are about to present is a bit of a dog's breakfast, but all will be good because you are an exquisite presenter, right? You have been through countless rounds of presentation training and with your amazing-looking slides – polished and refined by your in-house design team – you've got this.

You are confident you can deliver a performance so marvellous that nobody will notice that what is on the slides bears little resemblance to what you are saying.

Showtime myths

Two myths exist regarding the role of the presenter that we must address at this point.

Firstly, there is a school of thought that a great presenter with great-looking slides can save even an average presentation from going down the toilet. That may be true in some situations, but when you are presenting anything more than the most basic idea that someone can buy on the spot, this is not the case. What you put on the screen, what is on the slides, the story you tell and the content you leave behind *must* support you as the presenter and the audience to take your content forward. The greatest show will never be enough.

The second myth, accentuated by the first, is that you need to be an amazing presenter to sell ideas. And that is also not true.

Hang on, are you saying I can be a rambling nervous wreck and not get fired? No. But you don't need to be Tim Cook delivering an Apple keynote presentation in front of the world's media for the latest iPhone, or Barack Obama delivering a presidential speech, which is what many will have you believe.

It's easy to see why you might think being a great presenter is the key to getting your ideas to land and convincing your audience to partner with you, because this is where most 'presentation skills training' has been focused.

But this training wasn't developed with you or your needs in mind. It was designed for a completely different style of presentation, and it has led to an overemphasis on things that are not as critical for what you need. This can undermine and even destroy the confidence of an otherwise okay presenter, who is being told they are not good enough when they have adequate presentation skills but have woeful presentations that are losing them business.

You don't need the level of delivery prowess of, say, a CEO delivering an update to all staff and investors or presenting at a conference on a stage in front of thousands of paying guests or at annual events.

Here the delivery is critical to the impact of the message; the CEO is there to inform and inspire. The audience hangs on every word. The tone, pace, clarity and how each point is articulated really matter.

Take a CEO who looks nervous, stumbles and rushes through certain key points and appears to have forgotten elements of others; how will they go at instilling the required confidence in the team they lead and who are there to be inspired by them? For their most important presentations, CEOs of the country's top companies will have dedicated speech writers, and then weeks of rehearsals will follow with a coach to refine and fine-tune the delivery, because their delivery is everything.

How many of the presentations you deliver are ready in time for two weeks of rehearsals in front of a speaking coach? What would change if you had this luxury?

Quite frankly, not a lot, because your delivery isn't as important as theirs.

In the absence of really understanding what is happening, the solution to underperforming sales presentations and even under-performing sales teams is often to fund more presentation skills training: 'We need to make them more confident on their feet, more articulate and able to work the room better.'

But this misses the critical understanding of the nuances of striking the right balance of delivery, content and design for what you and your audience need. When you are delivering this book's style of presentation, what you present, and how you structure and curate the content carry as much, if not slightly more, weight and importance as how well you do on your feet as a presenter. Hence, this is a whole book dedicated to just this topic!

CLOSING YOUR GAPS

Since the rest of this book is all about closing the gap on what is missing for those who need presentations that help them sell and how to structure a winning presentation, let me clarify what is needed from you and your presentation skills that this book *won't* cover, so that if these are still gaps for you, you can seek out the right training and support for your needs.

You need to do more than read the slides

Let's talk about your role and what is required of you – the basic skills that, if not already in place, do still need to be worked on and are not part of what this book will cover.

The difference between a document and a presentation is you and your colleagues appear in the room (or on a screen for our much-loved online meetings) to narrate all or part of the content.

You are there to add value beyond just emailing the document through. At least, I hope that is why you are turning up, a bigger role than delivering the cupcakes.

Your role as the presenter is to bring what would otherwise be a flat document to life. In doing so, you can ensure that the key information is both seen and understood. You can emphasise, clarify, expand with additional information, share an example that can't be documented or left behind and, of course, you can leverage your personal delivery style to enhance engagement and keep the audience focused when you need their attention.

You do need to be skilled enough to do more than read the slides; if your audience is old enough to read, they don't need you there just to narrate what they can read in their own time. And you do need to be able to manage your nerves and not crumble at the first tricky question or, as I have seen – sadly, more than once – leave the room mid-presentation when the pressure overwhelms you. Your presence and how you hold and manage the room, as well as how you leverage the technology and environment to support you and how well you know your content and manage the pace of the presentation to keep the audience following along, never too fast that you lose them and not so slow that they can become distracted and tune out – all of this is important.

> **You do need to be skilled enough to do more than read the slides; if your audience is old enough to read, they don't need you there just to narrate what they can read in their own time.**

A well-told story helps us to recall information, and you are the storyteller, there to get this story across and into the memories of your expectant audience.

There is a skill to all of this, and learning and developing this does matter, just not as much as many would have you believe. But still, you do want to invest time in becoming the best presenter you can; just remember this isn't everything and will never be all you need to win.

If you don't already have a good idea of how you come across when you present, there are a couple of simple ways to find out.

The first is to record yourself; even just an audio recording of your next presentation, with the audience's permission, will give you immediate feedback on your delivery style. You will hear your confidence, and the tone and the speed at which you deliver. You will also hear any subconscious phrases you use when you get nervous or lost in the presentation. All valuable insights to begin to work on your delivery. This, of course, has become easier now with the increase in online presentations. Make an effort to sit and watch yourself present when a meeting is recorded. As painful as it can be to see ourselves on the screen, there is no better way to learn where you can make small changes that will make a huge difference. You might be surprised at how many little things you do, say or repeat that you didn't realise you were doing.

Next, you can seek feedback from your colleagues who are with you when you present or a client to whom you have recently presented. The truth is that most people struggle to give really honest and constructive feedback in this area. My advice to make this easier and more valuable is to be specific in your request. Detail three or four areas you want feedback on – such as pace, tone, confidence and clarity of delivery – and then give them a simple 1 to 5 scale to choose from. Then ask for one thing you do really well and one thing they think you could improve. You can vary what you ask each person, and you will start to build a picture of where you can focus or get help.

The clearer you are on the areas you want or need to work on, the easier it will be to home in on the right support. Presentation skills training is a vast area, with many thousands of books, courses and trainers willing to take your hard-earned salary, and you already know my view that a lot of this isn't as relevant to you as they will tell you it is. Get clear on what you need first, and then seek the right level of support to close your personal gaps.

THE SILENCE

It's been 10 days since you presented, and there is only deathly silence. No questions, no follow-up. A quick check – did I block their number by accident? Have their emails been going to spam? What is happening over there? Should I call to 'check in'? Maybe hang out in the lobby to bump into them by chance?

When your audience returns to the three to five presentations they saw 10 days ago, how easy is it for them to:

▶ recall your key points?

▶ remember what each point meant to them and how it helped them move forward?

▶ find the supporting information that brings these key points to life?

▶ take out one, two or three slides that they can use to summarise everything you presented?

▶ present your ideas to others?

Can they become you?

At the end of the day, how well you know your content, how excited you are about your ideas, and how practised and rehearsed you are – none of these things matter if your ideas don't land for your audience, and if they don't connect with the content in such a way that they can now champion your ideas. This means constantly asking yourself if you have made it as easy as possible for them to become you.

> **None of these things matter if your ideas don't land for your audience.**

You don't want your audience to give up on your content after just one presentation.

The challenge is that they don't easily recall as much as you might think.

In the all-time classic sales methodology book *Spin Selling*, Neil Rackham shares his research into how much of a sales presentation gets recalled. Here is what he learnt:

▶ The average seller made eight key points during a presentation.

▶ Immediately after the presentation, potential customers could remember an average of 5.7 of these.

▶ One week later, more than half had been forgotten, and only 2.5 of the original eight remained.

And with this reducing recall went their enthusiasm to buy. Immediately after the presentation, customers gave high ratings for their probability of buying. However, after just a week, the average rating for those same customers indicated they were now unlikely to buy.

Firstly, an average of eight points for a presentation would be a delight to see. (I have seen that many points on a single slide, but we will address this later.) The point Neil is making, supported by his research, is that just because you presented doesn't mean it was understood, can be recalled and has increased your chances of getting the win you desire.

After just one week, only two key points could be recalled.

Let me ask you this:

What if there are only two points that could be recalled from your last presentation? Have you made it clear what these should be? And made them stand out and easy to find?

If you haven't, you are hoping of all the points you made – and I am going to guess there are probably more than eight – that the most important ones just happen to be the ones that make it through.

Structure for you and them

You might think that after seeing your presentation just once it would be impossible for them to know everything about what you do, your products, services and ideas, and that there is no way they can take this and do an effective or even half-decent job of presenting this to others.

And that is the challenge that can only be overcome by how you structure your presentation and curate your content to not only support you in the delivery but also make it as easy as possible for someone to champion your ideas when you are not there to fill in the gaps.

Unless you are selling a simple solution and you have the decision-maker in front of you every time so you can close the sale there, you must learn how to empower your audience to take your key points and sell these on your behalf.

The Hopeful Presenter relies on the good fortune that something sticks or there is someone in the audience who either cares enough or knows enough to carry their ideas forward. The Strategic Storyteller constructs their story to make it clear what is important and to make it easy to find what information and slides support the selling of their ideas.

When you are selling solutions that contain multiple elements, connecting products to form campaigns, when you are selling strategic ideas that solve complex problems, such as multi-layered digital solutions with multiple sources of data and different service offerings, and when there are third parties evaluating your presentations on behalf of others, this is when the game changes significantly, and so does the nature of what you have to deliver.

With all of these, it is unlikely you will present once, have all stakeholders in the room and receive the go-ahead on the spot. Closing the sale at that moment just isn't going to happen.

You might present to the agency acting on behalf of the client, and the client only sees a fraction of what you presented, maybe a slide or two. Within the agency, multiple roles will pour over your slides and pick them apart before the client ever hears about or sees any of your content. Within the client team, they take the agency work and cut this down further to share for feedback, buy-in and sign-off.

All of this time, what you delivered once is having to continue to convey the points you made to people who have never seen you present. This is the game-changing difference between selling and presenting to win. Your presentation has to do a lot more work after you leave for you to win.

If the first person you present to struggles to recall just 30% of what you presented, and then on top of that you make it challenging, if not impossible, to find the critical points in your presentation and to find slides that are easy for them to present on, you diminish the enthusiasm for your idea – and with that goes your chances of staying in the game.

How well are you doing?

Find a recent presentation, one where you were looking to land critical information, sell a strategic idea or similar. Put the presentation onto slide sorter view:

- How clear is your story if you just read the titles?
- Now decide which are the three most important slides; yes, just three. (It should just be one, but we will get to that.)

And then give each of these three slides a score from 1 to 5 for the following:

- How well do just these slides land the main points of the presentation?
- How well do the headings convey the critical point of the slide?
- How clearly do they show how you solve a specific problem for the audience?
- How easy is finding the essential point on the slide after the heading?
- How well does the information on the slide flow logically from the header to the next point on the slide?
- What do you want someone to take away from this slide? How likely is it they would say that if they were presenting this slide without you?
- How many slides could your audience use to present your idea without you there to explain them?

The slides you want your audience to find and use easily are the ones that sell your idea on a page and clearly state the benefits you deliver through the way you solve their problem.

Make it clear what you want them to find

You might wonder, *How do I know what slides they will need?* The truth is you won't know exactly what slides they need, but you can make it abundantly clear to them which slides you think are the most important and they should use in the way you construct your slides and bring your presentation together.

The slides you want them to find and use easily are the ones that sell your idea on a page and clearly state the benefits you deliver through the way you solve their problem. These should be clear and present in every presentation where there is any chance you won't get what you need in the first showing.

Part I: Conclusion

Gaining insights into what is and isn't working in what you are presenting can be very difficult. Few will tell you what they really think, not because they are being difficult or dishonest but because it is hard to provide this type of feedback. It is often seen as quite personal: 'Look; your baby is really a bit ugly.' They know you have slaved over this content, and worked hard on pulling something together to answer their wants and meet their expectations, and so it can feel like they are bursting your balloon and deflating your enthusiasm to unleash the feedback that would actually help you improve.

And to compound this, there is very little material in the form of books, training or coaching geared to help you, built for your line of work that you can have confidence in.

So while this part might have been painful to read in places, and it may have even felt like I was looking over your shoulder or sitting in your presentations, you are now well equipped to advance.

To make changes, you have to understand the challenges showing up for you so you can work on overcoming whatever is getting in the way of your great ideas winning.

In fact, if you have taken a moment to reflect and complete the exercises, you will have formed a very clear picture of what is working and what isn't, and you will probably have already started to think about the changes you can make to master the art of winning as a Strategic Storyteller. And that is before we have explored what is coming up in part II, which is how you elevate every presentation to be a winning one.

Here are the 10 challenges that can stop even the best ideas from winning:

- ▶ Every presenter should start by knowing who the audience is for this presentation; it can't be 'everyone that might show up'.

- ▶ You have to meet the audience's wants and needs – their needs are where you will find a real connection.

- You have to solve their problem; a presentation without a problem to solve is a presentation without a purpose.

- You will always have more content than you need; it is, therefore, critical to know how to structure and control the flow of your content to land only what is needed and nothing more.

- You don't want to be peddling raw ingredients. Combining elements increases both the value and utility of what you have to offer the audience. You want to make it as easy as possible for them to buy you, and that means putting on the chef's hat and creating some tasty dishes from all your lovely ingredients.

- Too many presentations start in the detail and hope to join this together in a clever conclusion, but often the audience is lost long before the chance to do this materialises. Layering content to start with the highest level and most important points is a much better strategy for retaining both engagement and understanding.

- Beware product names, jargon and internal language that can creep into your slides and pollute your content. Your audience doesn't know what all of these things mean, and your job is to connect, not confuse.

- Every presentation needs a structure in place before you become overwhelmed with content or try to organise sections in the final few hours. Learning how to tell a flowing story built around clear navigation and a singular narrative is key.

- The spotlight can't always be on you. The goal is not to spend an hour sharing how great you are or ticking off the list of industry buzzwords. Ensure there is a balance to avoid boredom or bewilderment.

- Even the greatest presenter can't save an average presentation. Presentation skills are generally overrated. What you present really matters in winning presentations.

A winning presentation is one that supports both you and the audience in delivering your content.

INCREASE YOUR CONFIDENCE THROUGH THE THINGS YOU CAN CONTROL

Now you know what is needed and where your gaps are, you can stop beating yourself up over the things that probably don't matter as much as you thought and start to focus on the presentation (before doing another presentation skills course aimed at making you a presidential-style speaker), and believe that you have great products, strategies, ideas and solutions, and they deserve a better vehicle for their delivery.

You can now start to focus on the things you can control, the things you can change right now to improve your outcomes. There is nothing more empowering than taking control of your own destiny and outcomes.

And while it's true I don't know how great your ideas actually are, I do know that an average presentation will undermine a great idea and that a great presentation can elevate even the most average idea into a winning position.

Based on this, I know where I would put my focus.

Coming up is how to use the second part of this book, what it takes to create a winning presentation and the steps to guide you through doing exactly that.

Part II

CREATING WINNING PRESENTATIONS

HOW TO USE PART II

In part I, I covered the challenges that threaten to derail the best presenters and ideas. It is time to change gears and get into what it takes to overcome these. What moves a Hopeful Presenter forward to become a Strategic Storyteller?

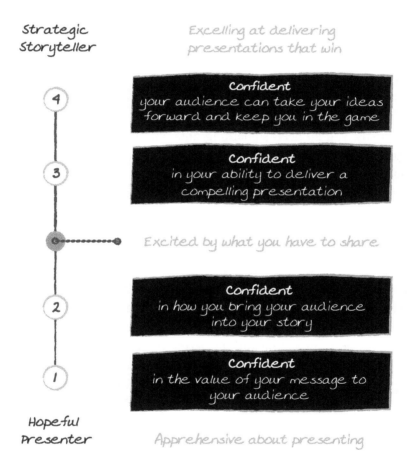

Strategic Storyteller — Excelling at delivering presentations that win

4 — **Confident** your audience can take your ideas forward and keep you in the game

3 — **Confident** in your ability to deliver a compelling presentation

Excited by what you have to share

2 — **Confident** in how you bring your audience into your story

1 — **Confident** in the value of your message to your audience

Hopeful Presenter — Apprehensive about presenting

The rest of this book is dedicated to exploring my 12 tools that have been carefully refined over the last 15-plus years to address your specific needs and to help you go on this journey.

Before you start on part II, to come is a quick overview of what you can expect, what this content will teach you and what it won't, along with an overview of what each of the next four chapters covers. I believe you will get the greatest benefit from going through all four first, but I appreciate you might be champing at the bit to get some answers to specific challenges bugging you right now.

WHAT THIS ISN'T AND WHAT IT IS

It's not another process

In my experience, most teams have quite enough processes, and the last thing an account manager, strategist or creative needs is to have to learn another one. So you won't be finding a '12 steps' approach that locks you into my way of doing things.

It is 12 independent tools for good reasons.

Firstly, you all need something different, and this means you can grab the tools that make the greatest impact on your work and help you move forward the most, and give less time and attention to areas where you are already strong or have an approach that works for you. The only thing I would say here is that just because you have a hammer and you can put in the nails and the screws, it doesn't mean you have the best tool for the job. My screwdriver might feel clunky to start with, but once you get the hang of it, you will see how much more effective it is on the screws and the hammer on the nails. So, what I am saying is, if it feels a little odd to start with, give it a go before you go back to your old ways, which might not be the better way.

The world of creating and delivering presentations is already surrounded by a world of process and, in many cases, already too many steps and gates. To be successful and helpful for you, this approach has to work within whatever sales, strategy and creative process you have. And it will; this doesn't replace any of that, but it can probably enhance quite a bit of it, and you will be able to quickly work out how each tool slots into your existing ways of working.

> **The world of creating and delivering presentations is already surrounded by a world of process and, in many cases, already too many steps and gates.**

Although each tool can work on its own, they are also cleverly designed to work incredibly well together. So if you do want something to guide you at each stage and you do like mastering different levels by applying your learning in stages, you will enjoy every aspect of the program.

Finally, I know you won't stick to a process even if I give you one.

It's not a fixed way of doing things

Okay, I do have some strong points of view and, as you have probably already sensed, I am not going to hold back in sharing these to help you become a better presenter. But the purpose of giving you tools to work with is to give you some freedom and latitude to make these your own and make them work for you.

Over the years of sharing this work, I have been surprised, amazed, blown away and, at times, a little nervous about how people have adapted my thinking to work for them. Initially, I didn't like people changing things or adapting them. But now, I love this. I love the idea of empowering you with what I know works, the approach to overcoming the biggest barriers, and then seeing where you take it.

In writing this and taking what has been workshop-style training for many years, I have fully embraced the idea of providing direction to empower you and help you avoid the potholes, along with the depth to know why this matters and the critical steps that are important, before setting you free to make this work for you in your world.

The real-world application of my work has always been a founding principle of everything I do. It's not what happens in the classroom; it's what you take away and can apply right away to make a difference at your desk that matters. This book is written to be on your desk and by your side whenever you need it; it is not a read once, be inspired and move on kind of book.

It's not about you

By now, you might have picked up that this book is not about how you present, public speaking, the use of a PowerPoint pointer, standing versus sitting and so on.

It is about what you present, the structure of the content you have and how you use slides to both help you and your audience understand, recall and present your ideas. This is the gap that desperately needs closing, and one that is stopping so many from making sales. In my view, it's so important that this entire book is focused on just that one aspect of presenting.

Now the benefit of this is that it also helps you become a more confident presenter, because the confidence or lack thereof in what you have to present is one of the factors that leads to nervous and rambling presenters. It will also help with running over time, missing key points and getting lost in your own content – other factors that can impact a presenter's confidence and ability to present effectively.

It's not a slide design course

Again, slide design is an important aspect of gaining and keeping your audience's attention, but which image library to use, choosing the right image sizes, cropping images to fit on slides, font choices, template design and how to use slide transitions are not topics for this book.

It's not a crash course in strategy

Yes, I do have many years in senior strategy roles, but this is not a strategy book; this isn't about how to come up with the audience insight or identify a new market, write a product, brand or marketing strategy or write strategic briefs for the creative team. This starts when you have something you want to share with others and need to get them to buy into or even buy your strategy, ideas, products or solution.

It is about increasing your skills to make more of the things you can control

The focus is on what you and your creative and strategic colleagues can take control of to give you the very best chance of taking the content you come up with and sharing this with others in a repeatable, consistent and winning way.

THE 12 SETS OF TOOLS ARE CONTAINED WITHIN FOUR TOOLBOXES

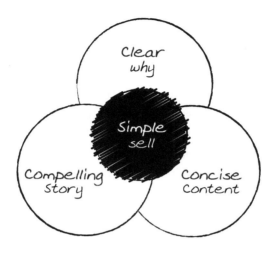

Each of the next four chapters covers one of the four toolboxes – Clear, Concise, Compelling and Simple – and takes you through the three sets of tools within that toolbox. These are arranged in order to highlight how they can build on each other, should you choose to use them all.

These four chapters cover the following:

- ► Be **Clear** about why this presentation exists, who it is for and what matters to them. Read this chapter to learn:
  - How to define **Who** matters most to you. Who is your audience?
  - How to discover the audience's **Needs** and what matters to them.
  - Why understanding the problem to be solved and the **Change** that you see as being possible is critical to every presentation.

- ► Be **Concise** in the organisation and visualisation of the content and being able to turn *every* presentation into a single page. Read this chapter to learn:
  - How to **Organise** all of your content to increase its value and utility.

- How to **Optimise** the flow of information to make it easier to present and easier for your audience to follow.
- How to **Visualise** your entire presentation on a page.

▶ Be **Compelling** through the story that is told to bring the audience into your content and connect them emotionally to what you have to offer. Read this chapter to learn:

- How to **Structure** your presentations around a three-stage story arc designed specifically for this type of presentation that will bring the audience into your story and help you navigate them to your resolution.
- How to ensure that the **Soundbites** of your narrative land the key points you need your audience to remember.
- How to refine your content so that the **Spotlight** isn't just shining on you.

▶ Being **Simple** is the ultimate goal for a Strategic Storyteller who wants to be armed with the highest-level view of their work, prepared to share this with anyone in any situation while ensuring others are able to take their ideas forward, even if they never see a slide. Read this chapter to learn:

- How to create an exciting and descriptive **Plot** that captures your entire story and creates a sense of anticipation.
- How to summarise the **Plan** for how you get from the problem to the resolution at the simplest level with the most powerful points at the ready.
- How to emphasise your impact, the **Potential** you bring that establishes why *this* presentation matters to them.

Logic to the layout

The tools are laid out to follow a logical order that starts from the moment you get a brief, conceive of an idea or begin to think about a solution you could create or take to market – long before the first slide has been created. They then take you right through to the last few minutes before you step up to present, and the final check before unleashing your content on the world.

These stages can vary from hours to days, weeks and sometimes months. So, at first glance, it can look like there are a lot of new steps to apply to a single presentation. However, when you work through them in the real-world application, applying them as you work through the many phases of developing your presentation, and particularly when you become practised at their application, you will wonder how you ever worked without them. How do I know this? It has been played back to me countless times by those who have been through this training.

WHO THIS IS FOR

As you will understand as you read this book, it has been written with a very specific audience in mind. An audience I know well and have spent many years working with, seeing hundreds of presentations from, coaching and now training. However, this book tackles taking any of the following types of content and helping you create a presentation when you need to convince the person you are presenting to do something with your content, when you don't get the 'win' on the spot.

This applies to:

▸ content that explains what products and solutions you have

▸ strategic thinking and ideas born from this work

▸ ideas you have developed either in response to a request or that you have decided the world needs and are wanting to share; 'proactive ideas', as they are often labelled

▸ a solution that could include any and all of these, where you have brought together multiple things into one presentation, probably quite a large one, that you now want to get your audience to buy into and take forward.

There are many ways to describe things and label them. If the work you do sounds anything like this and you need to create presentations that can determine whether or not that work gains traction with a certain group of people, you will find something of great benefit in the pages ahead.

Let the journey begin.

TOOLBOX 1:
GETTING CLEAR

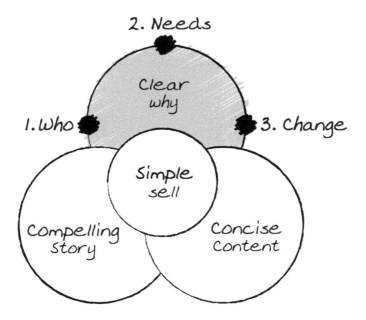

CLEAR

JUST IMAGINE ...

You know why you are creating this presentation.

You are clear about who this is for and what matters to them. You have a view of what could happen and how bad things could get without your solution, and you are clear on the overall change you see as possible.

As a result, as your solution comes to life, you can clearly articulate the actual value you can bring to your audience while filtering the content to ensure you take your audience on a journey from the problem to your resolution. You show how the change you envisaged as being possible is delivered through the story you are telling. Your audience feel like they are a part of that story, and it is precisely for them. You know exactly what they need, you share a view on what's possible and they want to go on this journey with you.

It is clear to you, and you are making it clear to them why this presentation matters. It is a presentation with a purpose.

That is what it means and what it feels like to have a high level of clarity.

What can we sell today?

So many presentations are created from great content, ideas and solutions but without knowing who the preesentation is for, and what matters to them, what they need from the presentation, and without the right level of clarity and understanding of the problem that needs to be solved.

When this is the starting point, a bunch of issues creep into your content and, before you know it, into your slides.

And when it comes time to present, hope appears in the form of:

- ► I hope our ideas resonate with someone in the audience.
- ► I hope we have something they need.
- ► I hope they can see how we can solve a problem for them.

The start of forming a strategic story

Getting clear on whom this is for, what is at stake and what's possible doesn't just set a presentation up for success from the outset; it serves as a guide through the entire process.

CLEAR

A few minutes working through this can save hours of back and forth and a great deal of frustration in the later stages when you are trying to decide what content fits, what the key points are and if the solution is right, as well as where to edit to refine the story. This is the very start of forming a strategic story, a winning story, and is a step you shouldn't skip if you want to move from being a Hopeful Presenter to a Strategic Storyteller.

Confidence in the clarity

When you work to create presentations that have this level of clarity, you increase your confidence in the value of your message to your audience, and their confidence in you as you demonstrate why this matters to them.

You have more confidence in how you bring your audience into your story, and how everything connects to take the audience on a journey from how bad things could get to how you can take them to a Better Place, not just resolving their surface problem but also increasing your content's relevance and their emotional connection to it so you can have a meaningful impact as you deliver against their underlying fears.

You know the point of the presentation and can already see the value in what you can deliver, even though you have yet to create a single slide.

In this chapter on getting Clear, I cover how to work through the following:

▶ **Who matters to you – this is your audience.**

 – Who do you need your content and story to connect with?

 – How can you determine the smallest number of people with the most significant impact on what you need from this presentation?

▶ **What matters to them – their wants and needs.**

 – How you can change your perspective to see the world through their eyes so you can feel what it's like to be in their role?

- — What do they want to see from you? What needs do they have, and what underlying fears and insecurities exist that, if you could show how you can resolve these, would connect your content and story with more significant relevance and a deeper emotional connection?

▶ **What is the change you see as possible?**

- — What is the problem that needs solving and the benefit you bring? And without your solution, how bad could things get for this audience? What's the worst that can happen based on your knowledge and expertise in this area?
- — What do you believe is possible, and what is the most significant change you can deliver?

Getting Clear is about Who, Needs, Change, the first three tools; that is easy to remember, right?

Toolset #1: Who matters to you

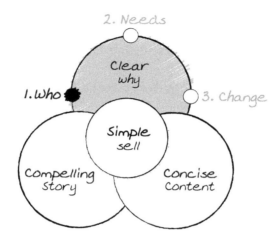

'Everyone' isn't an audience.

When you create a presentation without an audience in mind, several critical issues creep into your content from the outset. These become so intertwined and deeply ingrained in the structure's core that trying to resolve them later becomes difficult, time-consuming and sometimes impossible.

The presentation becomes generic, stuffed with content 'that might appeal to someone'. You don't know how to decide what should be left out.

As content comes in from around the organisation, each person makes a seemingly valid point for that slide going in. The committee of contributors builds the story by stealth, slowly eroding any semblance of coherence until the point of the presentation isn't clear at all.

It is considerably more challenging to stitch together a story that brings the audience in and makes them feel this is a story specifically for them when you have written it for everyone or anyone who might turn up on the day, when you hope that what you have might somehow find a friendly advocate who sees some value in at least one part of your content. It has become a Frankenstein presentation, clearly made up of different sections that don't neatly join, connect and flow; there is no glue or connecting thought to guide how any of this could and should relate or how it solves anyone's problem.

It is unclear to you – and even more perplexing to those sitting through it – what this is all about and what is essential for them to take note of. It has become a presentation for everyone, connecting with no-one.

Your presentation can't be for everyone. Ever.

Ken Haemer, Presentation Research Manager at AT&T, has been quoted as saying:

> Designing a presentation without an audience in mind is like writing
> a love letter and addressing it 'to whom it may concern'.

Given that love letters aren't so popular anymore, let me modernise this for you. Would you create a profile in an online dating app such as Tinder with a like-to-meet setting of 'everyone'? No, you wouldn't, so let's stop making presentations for anybody who might show up.

Your presentation can't be for everyone. Ever.

THE MORE YOU AIM FOR EVERYONE, THE LESS YOU CONNECT WITH ANYONE

Seth Godin, author of *This is Marketing* and some 20 other bestselling books, is very clear on this point: 'the book written for everyone sells no copies; we think we're designing and selling to everyone, but that doesn't match reality. It makes no sense at all to dumb down your best work to appeal to the long-time bystander when the bystander isn't interested.'

In another of his books he talks about what he calls the 'smallest viable audience, not everyone', the idea that you want to find the smallest number of people who are most interested in what you have and ensure there are just enough of them to deliver what you need. Then you talk directly to them and listen only to their feedback, not the people who aren't buying what you are selling.

To further this point, when Elizabeth Gilbert wrote her travel novel *Eat Pray Love*, she wrote the book for one specific person, a friend who could not come on the trip with her. Her book, written to a single person, has sold over 12 million copies and has been translated into 30 languages, with a movie version starring Julia Roberts that delivered over $200 million in box office takings. Not bad for a book written to just one person!

This is a core marketing principle: know your audience and talk specifically to them. Ignore everyone else. This exercise will enable you to determine who matters most to you.

What or, more importantly, who will keep you in the game?

Let's establish a basic principle: when you present anything that won't be approved, signed off on or bought on the spot, you need your content to have a life beyond this first presentation.

You might only present it once, but to get any follow-up – whether that is in the form of feedback right through to direction on the next steps – your content will be reviewed, cut down and shared with others, perhaps several times before you hear anything. When this is the case for your presentations, there are two crucial questions to ask yourself:

► Who matters most?
► Who can keep you in the game?

What this means is thinking about:

► Who can champion your ideas and will do the work to keep your content, thinking and ideas being considered and included in their recommendations so you stay in consideration and remain in the game? Who will connect your content to others after you leave?

The smallest number of people with the most significant impact

Think of it like this. After you finish presenting, you place your content on the table on a memory stick. It is there, sitting, waiting. As you leave the room, who will pick it up? Who is going to own taking your content forward from this point?

If no-one picks it up, what happens next? Precisely nothing. Perhaps you were entertaining, maybe this has helped you stay top of mind, but your content isn't going anywhere but in the bin when the cleaner clears the table later today. It's game over for this one.

To assist you in crafting a compelling story that connects your content with your audience, you need to determine the smallest number of people who can have the most significant impact on what happens next for you and your content.

You need to know who will be playing these three key roles:

▶ Who is best placed to take your content forward?

▶ Who can influence them and the person with the problem you are solving?

▶ Who has a problem that needs solving?

There might be many people in the room on the day or who you think might see your content after you leave. But this is who matters most for this presentation; this is whom your story needs to connect with. And the goal is to find the smallest number of people with the most significant impact in these roles. **That is your audience.**

Who is in these roles will vary depending on what you are presenting; that is, the complexity, value, scale in terms of a couple of weeks to a multi-year proposal, and the expertise required to evaluate your ideas. Each presentation you deliver will have different roles that make up your audience.

DETERMINING THE THREE KEY ROLES – YOUR AUDIENCE

It can be helpful to imagine these as seats around a table; you are at the table, sharing the story that contains the solution they all need, a confident position to imagine yourself in. But you are not the hero; they are. Your job is the guide, helping them to find their way to a Better Place, a place you know exists and you wish to guide them to.

There are three other seats around your table. These are occupied by:

▶ the Connector

▶ the Influencer

▶ the Impacted.

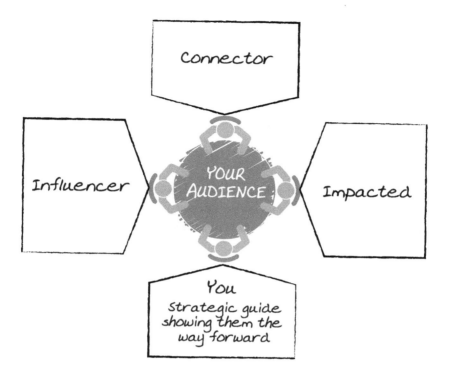

Any other people who may be in attendance are off to the side. They are present in the room, part of the wider audience; they hear and see everything and can ask questions. They may be able to lean in and whisper in the ear of someone at the table, but they are not in a position with the same importance to you as those you have invited to be with you around this imaginary table.

Your aim is always to determine the smallest number of roles with the most significant impact on keeping you in the game: to take your ideas forward, give you directional feedback, present to others on your behalf or include you in their recommendation.

Of the three positions, only one *really* needs to be in the room: the Connector. You must bring the Connector into your story and have them connect with your content and give them what they need to go on and do the job you need them to do. But thinking about and being able to see the world through the eyes of the other two will help shape your content.

A critical part of your job is to make it as easy as possible for the Connector to take what you present and make it their own; that is, to find what they need to do their job. Who is doing that next round of internal work for you and sharing your content if it doesn't connect with anyone? The answer is no-one. If there is no Connector present, there is no point presenting because there is no-one to carry your message forward.

> **A critical part of your job is to make it as easy as possible for the Connector to take what you present and make it their own; that is, to find what they need to do their job.**

Let's look at the three positions and how you determine who is sitting where on your imaginary table.

The Connector

Sitting opposite you is the person you need the most, the Connector.

A particular role type, position, level of expertise or, in a few cases, seniority might define this, but more often than not, they are *not* the most senior person; that is a trap to be very wary of.

You need to establish what role could represent your Connector for this presentation. Who will take what you present and be the guardian of your content? Who will find the slides that need to go into a more extensive presentation that your ideas might only be a small part of? Who will take others through your ideas and gather feedback?

Do not assume this is the person with the most grandiose title or the most fabulous swagger; think about who will take what you present, interpret it, cut it down to suit their needs and carry it forward. Who will do the work? Very rarely is that the most senior person or the strategist; they often play other roles.

The Connector in action

The Connector may well have briefed you and be the one who wants this to happen. During the presentation, they may be exuberant, nodding and giving reinforcement and reassurance. These people are like seals being thrown fish, clapping along and excited for what might come next. Be careful of their overt positivity. They still need to convince others, and you must help them do this; otherwise, they are just a performing seal with one trick.

The key Connector questions are:

▶ Who in the room is best placed to connect your story to others and keep you in the game?

▶ How can you make it as easy as possible for them to do this?

A person or a role?

At this point, you might be thinking, *Is this a person or a role?*

You can define those around your table as either a person or a role. The degree to which you differentiate between the two will depend on the specifics of your relationship and the knowledge of who will be in your presentations.

In my experience, it is often more beneficial to remain at a role level, knowing that the role is where your connection needs to be, even though you might be unsure of precisely who from that level will attend your presentation. Let's say your Connector is in a Trading Director role, but several of those work across the area your presentation covers. Knowing the role will be enough to guide you through creating a more meaningful connection, even though you don't know who specifically will show up.

With each of these positions, you want to create a hierarchy; if 10 people are attending your presentation, keep working up to define the role that has the most power in that position, *not simply the most seniority*, which we will cover in a moment.

And yes, there may be a couple of roles that could be your Connector, such as a Trading Director and a Strategist who can carry elements of your ideas forward. You want to consider them both as you develop your story.

The critical part of this, however, is to keep challenging yourself to keep your audience as tight as possible. Once you let your mind wander to catering to all 10 roles that might show up, you are presenting a generic set of slides that you are *hoping* might appeal to someone. That is what you must work on avoiding through this exercise.

The Influencer

On your left is the person who influences the other two positions.

This person has the ear of both the Impacted and the Connector. They may be a subject matter expert, a budget holder or someone who these two people trust. When you think about the role with the most significant influence, consider what gives that role influence, and what perspective they bring that the other two roles don't have.

In a moment, you will learn how to get beyond this and uncover their broader motivations, but these two elements help define what roles will occupy this seat for this presentation.

You need to be aware of this role and think about how you are catering to their specific motivations, and think through what their objections and challenges to your ideas could be as you develop the content (not when you are on your feet presenting).

The Influencer is most likely to be the negative one, the black hat. They will think about the angles through which they might challenge your ideas.

Consider how you can give them what they need to hear or see before, during and after the presentation. Only some things need to be or should be addressed in your core narrative.

This can become distracting both for you as the presenter and the broader audience if these almost sidebar conversations don't flow with the main content and story you are presenting. If you are clear on what your Influencer wants to know – let's say they will have specific questions about your process, how you manage data security, or specifics around a deal structure – that could be distracting to the idea you want to get everyone across, cover this upfront and say you have this information ready for them and will have separate follow-up conversations to cover these areas. Or send these details over before or after you have presented.

The key is managing their expectations; you don't want them sitting there, getting increasingly agitated when they can't see how their questions will be resolved.

The Influencer in action

During the presentation, the Influencers can be the quiet ones, slowly, secretly taking your ideas apart and finding all the holes. They may look uninterested most of the time, only springing to life when it's time for questions, having crafted the curly questions to fire at you to expose what they see as holes in your story. Be prepared upfront by thinking through all the things they might want to know and have a plan for dealing with them as best you can.

The key Influencer questions are:

▶ Who can influence the decision to progress with you?

▶ How can you prepare to solve their potential questions and requests?

The Impacted

On your right is the person impacted by a problem they would like solved.

The problem will belong to the client in a typical client–agency relationship. They are directly impacted by this and want it solved. They bear the most significant pain of this problem. The agency is working on the client's behalf to source partners who may be able to help. They do not have the problem, just the task of helping to solve it. If it remains unresolved, they may have consequences, but they are not directly impacted by the ongoing challenge of having this problem.

You may never meet the person with the problem, the Impacted, during the entire sales cycle or present directly to them. Still, ultimately you need to demonstrate how you can solve the problem for them, so understanding this problem more deeply is very important.

The Impacted in action

If they are present during the presentation, the Impacted may be indifferent. They may be giving little away but taking many notes. They want the best solution and are constantly asking themselves, 'Does what I am seeing help me solve this problem? Does this help me move forward?'

Any questions will be well considered; they want to cut through the fluff to decide whether or not you can help them. Their interest and motivations are generally the cleanest: show me how you help me move forward and to a Better Place.

The key Impacted questions are:

▶ Who has the problem that you need to solve?
▶ How clearly can you demonstrate the benefits you bring and the change you see as being possible?

*

Whether selling through an agent or directly, these roles exist regardless. In a direct client presentation, your client in the room – say, a media manager or marketing manager – is your Connector. They are now representing the owners of the problem – the Impacted – who could be a product owner within a specialist area or even a CEO business owner or a dealer principle in a smaller client who has called on the marketing folk to help them solve a problem.

EVERYONE WANTS THE PROBLEM SOLVED

Even though the problem is felt most acutely by the Impacted role, everyone at your table will have an eye on whether what they are seeing helps to resolve this problem, and to what extent it does so, how significant is the change and, therefore, how much value they see in your ideas.

The Connector will be reluctant to take ideas forward if they can't see how this problem is being solved or if there is only little change and, therefore, value, and the Influencer will have a sharp eye on whether they can see any flaws in the argument or can't see how this change is possible.

Knowing your audience means you can:

▶ Bring the **Connector** into your story and give them what they need to get you what you want.
▶ Prepare to win over the **Influencer** by thinking about what they need to hear and see.
▶ Demonstrate the change you see as possible for the **Impacted** and those representing them in your audience.

A final word on the Connector

The Connector is one of the most important, least understood and, as a result, most frequently overlooked roles. In my experience, too much time and attention are placed on trying to influence decision-makers beyond your immediate and even secondary level of influence – far-off roles you know little about. You also may not know specifically which roles perform what aspects of the decision. You certainly don't get to meet or present your compelling story to them. So why spend so much time fussing over what they might think when you have no idea? This is also a problem when focusing on the most senior person who might attend, which I will address from a personal perspective in a moment.

Instead, you need to bring your focus to how you can help your Connector do the job of selling your ideas. That you can control.

PLAYING TO THE TITLES, NOT THE ROLES

The most senior person is rarely the Connector. They are not the ones cutting down the presentation, finding key slides and merging these into their broader story.

So many times, I see people present to the most senior person in the room like no-one else is there. And then they don't win and wonder why.

I have been that most senior person as a chief strategy office and agency MD and, let me tell you, it is super awkward. The team is there, they have done the work on the brief and will do the work to take this forward, and they are employed and empowered to make the call on what happens next, not me.

And yet most of the time the presenter is presenting, they are directing content and sales smiles to me. I try to deflect them onto the team by asking my own team what they think of certain points to signal that their view matters more than mine. And the presenter fails to get the hint as their eyes lock back onto me like a fly buzzing around at a BBQ. I have the same thought as I would in that situation; buzz off and leave me alone.

I turned up for the free muffins, a new notebook and because I might get asked for my POV by the team or the client. I have no material impact on the direction this takes after the meeting. The team are empowered and will make that call. I am, at best, a weak influencer should it get down to a marginal call, but to think I am the Connector is a big mistake. After this meeting is done, if I make it to the end, I am off and may never see this content or set of slides again. To present to me, alienate the team and fail to bring them into the story is a huge mistake. And it happens way too often. Stop it.

THE DEVIL *ISN'T* IN THE DETAIL

With the Connector, Influencer and Impacted roles, you won't always get everything spot on and, in some cases, you might make educated guesses on certain details. Here is the thing, an important little secret. **It doesn't matter.**

How accurate you are about each role is not as important as the change of perspective you get from doing this exercise. The critical point is not that you nail precisely what they are thinking at the very moment you deliver slide 64.

No, this is all about being able to change perspective; it is about seeing what you are presenting through the lenses of what these roles might need from you. Doing this shifts your focus from what you want to push out into the world to what they need to get you what you need, which is to stay in the game.

It is a subtle twist but an incredibly powerful change. What matters is how you curate your content thinking about what goes in and gets left out, what goes on the actual slides, how you unpack the details through to how you connect everything and tell a flowing story for *this* audience. The audience at your table.

Reducing your focus to the three roles and thinking about these for every presentation will make a dramatic difference to how you move forward from this point, even if the details are a little off. Remember, a book that was written for one person, *Eat Pray Love*, sold 12 million copies. When there is a focus to your story, you will be rewarded with a larger audience that cares about your content.

Who matters to you

Connector

They must be present in your presentation

Who can champion this content and these ideas, and do the work to keep you in the game?

Who will refine your content to go into a bigger presentation?
Who will take others through your ideas and gather feedback?
Who will present your content next?

Identify the one or two most impactful people who can do this.

How can you make it easy for them to take what you present and make it their own, and to find what they need to do their job while helping you?

Bring the **Connector** into your story, make it feel like it is just for them and give them what they need to keep you in the game.

Influencer

Armed and dangerous

Who can influence the decision to progress with you?

What is it that gives that role influence?

What perspective do they bring that the other two roles don't have?

Prepare <u>before</u> you present to give them what they need – either in the presentation, before or after it.

You don't have to present everything!

Prepare to win over the **Influencer** by thinking about what it is that they need to hear/see.

Impacted

Care but won't be there

Who has a problem that needs solving?

Typically the client or an MD/CEO within an SME
They own the pain of the problem and are most impacted by this.
Their motivations are clear – help me solve this problem.

They expect everyone 'representing them' to share their concern for this problem.

How are you helping them move forward?
How can you make the benefit you bring as clear as possible?

Demonstrate the change you see as possible for the **Impacted** and those representing them in your audience.

A MOMENT OF CHOICE

Do not skip this step. Or, to put this another way, if you want to skip this step, put down this book, because you are not ready for what comes next. You are not ready to move from a Hopeful Presenter to a Strategic Storyteller if you are not able to take this first step.

The accuracy is less important than the change of perspective. Your job is to guide the three people at your table, and imagining who they are will guide what you create so that it has focus and solves something for someone else before delivering what you need as a consequence.

Toolset #2: Needs: What matters to them

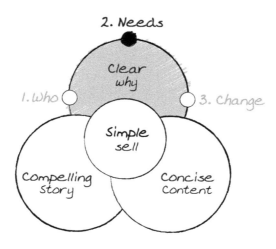

They feel like you are talking just to them.

We have established the roles that make up the audience for this presentation – that is who matters to you. Now we want to determine what matters to them, this tightly defined audience.

You want to get to know them in such a way that you can form a powerful connection with them, so that what you present stands out relative to your competition and they feel like you are talking just to them even though you might never have met them.

There are two powerful forces that will help with this: relevance and emotion.

Relevance increases attention. We know through countless advertising studies that the relevance of the advertising increases the attention consumers give it. A recent advertising study conducted by research agency Sparkler for the IAB in the UK concluded that 71% of consumers said relevance was key to advertising getting their attention. Relevance also had a positive impact on people's perception of quality.

The same holds true with your content, and you want attention when you are presenting.

Imagine if your content formed such a strong connection that your audience found it easy to remember and recall key points several days or weeks after you presented. The key to this is positive emotional experiences, and that is because emotion is a very powerful driver of memory, and how our brains receive, prioritise and store information. So, when you present a largely rational and expected response, the brain is frankly a little bored. I know that doesn't sound very scientific, but here is how the Queensland Brain Institute explains it.

One thing that helps make a memory robust is if it has strong emotional content. This happens because of the amygdala, which brain imaging studies have shown is activated by emotional events. This boosts memory encoding by enhancing attention and perception and can help memory retention by triggering the release of hormones, such as adrenaline and cortisol, to boost arousal.

While memories of a stressful event can be enhanced, stress tends to have negative effects on memory storage. Stress alters the way that our brain processes information, changing from a flexible, holistic approach to more rigid stimulus–response associations. This can change the nature of the memory stored, as well as what we recall under stress.

Imagine if your content formed such a strong connection that your audience found it easy to remember and recall key points several days or weeks after you presented.

What we have learnt from the advancement of science and the ability to see activity in the brain through improved technology in brain imaging is that positive emotional responses help forge stronger memories, whereas stress can negatively impact how we store and recall information. So we want to avoid creating stress when we are presenting. Those long, complex or overwhelming presentations that don't have a clear point or don't solve the audience's problem or are overtly pushing something the audience doesn't think they want or need can be stressful, and don't help build positive memories that aid recall.

When we think of positive emotions, it can be easy to think we need to tell jokes and use lots of photos of babies and cats doing funny things. However, a far more accessible and much safer approach for most business presentations is to demonstrate that you can deliver a meaningful change for them; that is, you can, through your narrative and story, highlight where you can reduce or resolve a fear they have, make them feel more secure in their role or your area of expertise, or help them to elevate their status as a thought leader, innovative thinker or trusted adviser.

When you do this, you solve their underlying needs, and that moves you from a rational connection to an emotional one.

UNCOVERING WHAT MATTERS TO THEM

Let's take a look at what you can uncover about your audience to increase both the relevance of your content and your emotional connection – forming more meaningful connections that elevate your content above your competition.

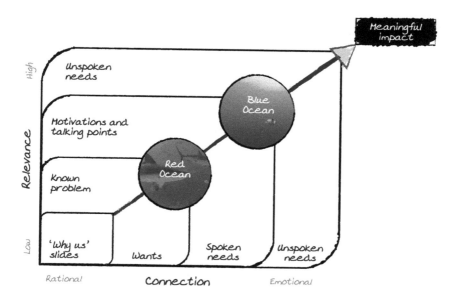

Consider the diagram above. If you don't think about the audience at all, you can be down in the bottom left corner with a deck that is full of 'why us' slides. Slides all about what you do. Incredibly rational, and potentially with very little relevance. You might hope to find some relevance as you present, but you haven't done anything to create it.

The next level is to be thinking about the known problem and what they want – this will often be covered in a brief, although it can still be overlooked or ignored. Now the risk here is that everyone else probably has the same information as you. So there is a very limited advantage here. Even though this elevates your connection and relevance, it's not where the win will be easy.

Then comes their motivations, talking points and spoken needs. These are things that are not written down, and not openly or widely shared; however, once understood they move you from a purely rational connection into the emotional space and with significantly more relevance and, therefore, attention to what you have to say.

Finally, we have the unspoken needs of the audience, or what I like to call their fears and insecurities. When you work on understanding these and, more importantly, tune your presentation to help resolve these in some way, you will be in a completely different space from everyone else, and your content will resonate with your audience as though you have written it just for them.

The first two sections lead you into what I call the Red Ocean. It is the bloody water where there are more sharks than fish; there is a feeding frenzy as everyone fights for what little food there is, and it is a competitive mess.

The upper two sections live in a very different territory. This is the Blue Ocean; there are very few predators here, the water is clear, and your idea can shine through and form a lasting and powerful connection.

> **When two or more products, ideas or solutions appear to be the same, the one that appeals to an emotional need will win over the ones that don't. And when none of them do this, price becomes the determining factor.**

When two or more products, ideas or solutions appear to be the same, the one that appeals to an emotional need will win over the ones that don't. And when none of them do this, price becomes the determining factor.

Where would you rather be?

Getting clear on what matters to them

There are two steps to achieve this level of understanding, the second building on the first:

1. Understand the type of people in the roles that matter to you – background, drivers and hot topics.
2. Understand what matters to them – their wants, spoken and unspoken.

This starts by forming a rich and powerful understanding of these roles to begin to uncover who these people are beyond the functional level, and what you want from them. To do this, create a persona for each role of interest to you; this is an overview of the stereotypical person in each role.

This isn't about the specific people. Although you can complete this exercise at that level as well, it's about having enough detail to be able to begin to see and feel the world through their eyes in their role. This forms the starting point for working through the Wants, Spoken and Unspoken Needs. This is where you can elevate your competitive advantage by crossing the threshold from rational, widely known and shared challenges to connect with the layers that live beneath.

What's it like to be them?

You are no doubt an expert in what you want to get across; you will almost certainly have an abundance of content to share. What will make this all the more powerful is being able to see and evaluate your content through the eyes of the audience, filtering for relevance and making subtle changes to the language, the level of detail and how you craft a story that can bring them in and help them feel it is a story they are a part of.

Successful American screenwriter Chad Hodge, in a *Harvard Business Review* article about the lessons from filmmaking in relation to creating business content that connects with audiences, said engaging people in your story is about helping 'people to see themselves as the hero of the story … Everyone wants to be a star, or at least to feel that the story is talking to or about him personally.'*

Screenwriters know that you don't start writing a movie script until you know whom you are writing for and what matters to them. It is a powerful lesson that holds true for your presentations as well. You need to make this about them, and for that, you need to get to know them a bit better than just a title or as one of your three most important roles that define your audience.

CREATING ROLE PERSONAS

So far, in defining the audience, you have learnt how to identify the roles you need your content to connect with through the three positions around your table. This exercise will guide you through another powerful change of perspective by creating a one-page persona for all of the roles you need to understand beyond the surface-level title and a basic understanding of what they do. You are essentially looking for the stereotypical attributes that define a role.

When this is done well, you will be able to connect your content to them in such a way that you make it feel like you are presenting just to them because, in essence, you are.

As you work through this, two things will probably become evident very quickly. At a role level, there are some very distinct differences in the backgrounds and motivations across different roles. And almost in contradiction to this, although actual titles may vary significantly across the industry, there are many common attributes within each role level – say, that of the senor trading function or the strategic leadership group – that will allow you to draw a very clear picture of this level and who you will be presenting to, even though you don't need to know the actual names of the people in these roles.

The persona has these core areas:

► their background
► their drivers
► their talking points.

---

* 'The Four Truths of the Storyteller', Peter Guber, *Harvard Business Review*, Dec. 2007.

I find it most helpful to do this next exercise at the role level, but you can also do this for a specific person you know will be in your audience if you prefer.

The benefit of working at a role level is you don't become caught up in the detail of a specific person. As a result, you will be less critical of whether something is exactly right, and less focused on the minute details that really don't matter. For instance, when thinking about their lifestyle, whether they drive a BMW or a Mercedes isn't as relevant as the fact they drive to work in their luxury car. When you know the person, you can get caught up overthinking this and wracking your brain trying to remember what the logo was on their car keys. What is needed here is enough depth to enable you to feel what it is like to see your work through the eyes of someone at this level with their knowledge, motivations and expectations.

> **The benefit of working at a role level is you don't become caught up in the detail of a specific person.**

On the following page is the template that will guide you through this exercise in detail, and you can download a copy here: www.davidfish. com.au/downloads/wp.

Here is a snapshot of what each section is designed to draw out and its role in helping you connect with them.

Background

Portrait and career

The first part of the background is to establish what defines people in these roles: who they are as people, how they came to be in these roles, what aspirations they have and what might be next for them.

This puts a stake in the ground. Are these wide-eyed 20-somethings or people in their 40s, experienced and worldly? You are positioning the role to give it context, so you can paint your own mental picture of these people. This will help with the rest of this exercise, and it will also help you step into this role more easily when you want to look at your presentation and your content through their eyes.

NEEDS

Template: **Role persona**

BACKGROUND

Portrait

Role title and a typical first name for this level.

What defines the typical person in this role, including age, lifestyle, where they live, and whether they drive or commute on public transport. Create a pen portrait of the typical person in this role or find an image online.

Photo

Career

How did they get into their current position, what might a typical path look like, and what aspirations do people in these roles typically have? Where next for them?

Interactions

What interactions do they have with your business and your products? How frequently do they come into contact with you, and how familiar are they with what you do?

DRIVERS

Motivation

What excites them, why do they do what they do, and what are their core motivations?

What is their role in evaluating your ideas and solution? What are they looking for based on what they are motivated by?

Interests

What is their level of interest, knowledge and experience with the area/topic of your presentation?

How keen are they to be in this conversation with you? What are they seeking to learn and know for growth and development versus what you want to share or want them to know?

Problems

What problems do they face within their role?

TALKING POINTS

Hot topics

What are the things they are talking about, the trends and the topics they love to engage in?

What wins them over and helps get a meeting or an idea across the line?

Things to avoid

What confuses, bamboozles or bores them?

When do they switch off, fail to show up or stop returning calls?

Give the persona an identity

Even though I advocate creating your persona at a role level, giving it a name and finding a picture that captures a typical person in each role will significantly help you understand whom you are presenting to and begin to tune your content accordingly.

A first name that embodies the generation and background and then a quick online search for a stereotypical image is all that is needed. Do they always dress formally or prefer t-shirts and sneakers? Do they have glasses that make them look smart or help them see? You know exactly what I mean! Young and fresh-faced or showing signs of 30-plus years in the industry?

This will bring your page to life and let you step into this role and connect with it more easily.

Interactions

The last part of the background section is to think about the interactions they have with your business and your products. How frequently do they come into contact with you, and how familiar are they with what you do?

Who are you to them, and how well do they know you?

This has a big part to play in how your Connector and your Influencer might view what you have to say, influencing the lens through which they are looking at you and what you will need to do to help them to help take your content forward.

If they only see you twice a year or even once a quarter, you can be sure that any internal jargon – your verbal shorthand and three-letter acronyms that might creep into your content – will likely confuse them. You know this secret code, but to them you might as well be presenting in a foreign language because they have no idea what is happening. However, if they see you twice a week, it is possible they know this secret code as well as you do.

If they are familiar with your business, there are many short cuts you can take in explaining your ideas; whereas if they are not, you must take the time to bring them carefully into your world, explaining and emphasising key points and avoiding the assumption that they know this as well as you do. That is a great way to lose them in the first five minutes and for them never to connect to a single word you said after that.

Drivers

Motivations (what drives them beyond solving the problem?)

The next section guides you to think about what people in these roles might be driven by; that is, their motivation and their interests.

What excites them, why do they do what they do and what are their core motivations?

What is their role in evaluating your ideas and solution? What are they looking for based on what they are motivated by?

What is their level of interest, knowledge and experience with the area or topic of your presentation?

How keen are they to be in this conversation with you? What are they seeking to learn and know for growth and development versus what you want to share?

> **What is their role in evaluating your ideas and solution? What are they looking for based on what they are motivated by?**

Their motivations will help you think about what they want to see from you beyond how you solve the problem. If they are motivated by status, award wins and how many views their content gets on LinkedIn, this will give you a very clear steer on what they will be looking for in your content. How does this elevate them? Could this give them fresh content to position them within the industry if this goes ahead?

If they can see how you are helping them in this regard, they will likely be ready to help you by supporting your ideas.

To be clear here: you have to solve the problem first and foremost, but if several solutions do this adequately, this becomes table stakes, and it can be almost impossible for a little self-interest not to creep in. It is human nature to consider: what does this do for me? Thinking about the motivations of your Connector and Influencer can, at the very least, keep you in the game long enough to get your ideas in front of the client, who, if they are the Impacted person, is looking critically at how you solve their problem, which is also a kind of self-interest!

Interests and problems

What excites you and your knowledge of this area may be vastly different to theirs.

Now, very few people think deeply enough about the interests, knowledge and experience of their audience and how this may be very different from how you see the world. In my experience and based on the feedback of those who have successfully worked with these templates, this can lead to some dangerous assumptions that result in significant disconnects.

Understanding this and reflecting on it as you curate your content and craft a story will help you make changes that you otherwise might not. You can tune your language, adjust the depth to which you need to move from high-level explanation to supporting detail, and add simple overview visuals or an analogy to help them remember key points that are brand new to them.

There are two things about presenting solutions and ideas that are worth reiterating:

▶ No-one will ever present anything to their peer group, seniors or a client that they don't fully understand. Ever. Period. And that includes anything on a slide that might trigger a question they can't answer. They will either remove that point from the slide or not use that slide at all. And if that was the only slide from your deck that was going to represent your idea, it's game over; you are not getting a call back this time.

▶ If there is something they need help understanding fully, are a little unsure about or need further validation of, it is doubtful they will go to great lengths researching this after you leave. You might get a call asking for further detail but, as you would know, some role levels don't like admitting they don't know or understand something, so if they can manage without you and can avoid the embarrassment of asking follow-up questions, they might move on without you.

It would help if you captured this level of detail in your persona to help you consider this as you craft your slides for this particular role.

You have to give them what *they* want and need from you, in their role, to do what they need to do next. You have to leave the presentation without a doubt that your Connector can confidently share what you have taken them through, even if that means creating specific slides to enable them to do that.

Understanding their drivers will give you a head start on this, as will the exercises coming up to discover their Needs and the transition from rational to emotional drivers.

Talking points

Hot topics and things to avoid

Everyone has their hot topics and things they would rather avoid. The hot topics draw you into a conversation, get you excited and light you up. The things to avoid can shut down conversations, embarrass people or cause discomfort if they are outside of their expertise or comfort zone.

You can see how beneficial it is to understand this before you put pen to paper; this can help you cut out jargon that can annoy your audience and include certain phrases and references you know are relevant and interesting to them.

This is a simple yet smart way to increase your cut through and your connection. Take the time to think about what these roles are talking about, what they are posting or commenting about on social media and when you see them visibly disconnect from conversation.

Understanding to application

You may recall I mentioned earlier that, in my experience, most people know more about their audience than they realise. This template aims to help you surface what you know and make an educated guess on what you don't think you know that well.

Yes, that's right, I said *guess* about the things you don't know that well. Use your experience to make a call and get something down and you won't be so far off that this makes things any worse than having a blank sheet where you would have built a hopeful presentation – hoping it resonates with someone in the room and hoping that someone cares enough to give you a call back. Very hopeful indeed.

The point of doing this work is to build a richer, more meaningful understanding than comes from just a job title or list of names attending your presentation. However, the benefit is not the understanding but the application of this process, how you leverage this understanding to connect your story and narrative to them, and to make it as easy as possible for them to do what they need to next.

'But we have a response to get finished'

Something I hear a lot at this point is: 'We don't have time to do more work upfront. We need to get into building responses as soon as the brief lands.' And I understand there are some significant time pressures in many areas.

Firstly, this doesn't have to be down tools, let's work out the audience before we do anything else. You can brief other departments, share what you know of the opportunity and so on, and then come back and reflect on the audience, the problem and how you now see the world through their eyes as the solution comes to life.

This can be done in less than half an hour, and if you work at the role level, each time you complete a persona you have it ready for the next time this role is your Connector or Influencer in a presentation.

And consider this. How much time do you waste going back and forth, trying to wrangle content, arguing over what should be left out, and trying to manage multiple stakeholders who all know what is best and want content included for every role that might show up?

Knowing just this much about your audience will enable you to cut through this and make a call on what is and isn't going to work in this presentation.

And what about the time spent responding to follow-up questions, if they happen, or even preparing a re-brief where you are asked to clarify so much it is an entirely new presentation, if such a luxury should exist?

A little bit of time upfront working through this can change the structure, narrative, slide layout and content and, as a result, the outcome of your presentation. This will both dramatically increase your chances of success and save you time down the road.

Coming up, you will learn how to take this foundational understanding to the next level to allow you to move from a rational connection to an emotional one. Having completed the personas first will set you up for this to be a much simpler but also a far more powerful exercise.

WANTS AND NEEDS: FROM RATIONAL TO EMOTIONAL

You can create a competitive advantage by crossing the threshold from rational, widely known and shared challenges to connect with the layers that live beneath all of this, which are defined by their underlying needs.

The path to emotional connection

Connecting your story to your audience's underlying needs means you can reframe how you deliver the content to highlight specific points and align your narrative in such a way that you hit their emotional hot buttons – a secret checklist of the things that are really important to an individual in a specific role, facing certain challenges. These hot buttons are ever present but never make it into a briefing document or get shared in open forums.

You have to go looking for them. They are always there, waiting to be found and, when solved, create a bond that is far greater than just aligning with what they have asked for or expect to see. You are now demonstrating how you can deliver much greater change from their current reality and the fears and insecurities that plague them personally. You are showing how you help them because you deeply understand what it feels like to be them and know how your ideas can deliver for them in their specific role. That is what understanding needs means.

No way of knowing?

It can be easy at this point to fall into the trap of thinking you have no way of knowing what is happening beneath the surface, or finding out what these underlying needs are. You barely know the person beyond their title and what you see of their role, which in many cases is actually very little beyond a few one-hour meetings and a couple of presentations each year. How could you possibly understand this level of depth about them?

With the work you have already done on defining the audience and developing a one-page persona for each role, this establishing framework now comes into its own. This will help you work through the next set of exercises as they work together to continue to enhance the picture. You will be surprised, if not amazed, at how much you do know and can uncover about your audience in the steps ahead.

Now, if you have skipped the first part of this chapter and haven't worked through who is in your audience and the personas for these roles, this will be more challenging, and I encourage you to go back and take the time to define the audience, and build out your perspective so you can enhance this with what they want and really need from you.

Discovering their emotional drivers

This next exercise will help you discover what lives within each of these three levels, each one building to reveal more powerful insights into these roles and how you can increase your relevance and your emotional connection.

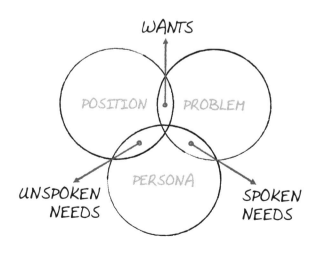

Consider each element of the preceding image:

▶ **Wants:** This starts with what your audience knows and tells you they want from you – this is generally shared openly and comes in a written brief. This is a combination of their position at the table – their role and what they want to be able to do their job – and how this intersects with what they want to see in respect of the problem being solved.

▶ **Spoken Needs:** Their Spoken Needs go to another level, a more personal level. This is where the persona, that insight into who they are, intersects with the problem; this is the start of a shift from what they want to fulfil their role at the table to what they personally need. This is where their motivations, relationships and talking points influence what they will say to you they need over and above the details shared in a written document such as a brief.

▶ **Unspoken Needs:** Their Unspoken Needs go to the most personal and emotive level, and are something you perceive to be true, not something you are likely to have been told is so. This lives in the intersection of their position at the table where what they are expected to bring, know and deliver, and their motivations, relations and talking points converge to create fears and insecurities. A place where judgement, status and meeting the expectations of others all reside. These needs go way beyond what is captured in any brief or requirements document, and even beyond the things you are told outside of the formal meetings when they confide in you what they need. These needs are not shared, but they can still be known to you. Solving these Unspoken Needs elevates you to a whole new place as you deliver an unexpected level of benefit and form an emotional connection that ensures you and your ideas stand out.

The aim of this exercise is to leverage what you have learned and can now understand by creating the personas of particular importance: those for the Connector and Influencer. You want to use these to put yourself in their role, to walk in their shoes and go beyond who they are to imagine what it is like to have their expectations, pressures, experiences and motivations, so you can explore what might lie just beneath the surface. How thin is the veneer of confidence when you feel what it is like to be them?

Wants

What someone wants from you is the easiest place to start. These are the things that are most commonly shared upfront and provided in both spoken and written form in documents such as a formal brief or requirements document. However, they won't just be shared with you; these are the known and expected requirements of anyone your audience engages with to help them. This includes the Impacted person wanting their problem solved.

Despite these not necessarily giving you any direct advantage, it is still important to get clear on the specifics and to capture these, so you have them to hand as you develop your presentation.

Even though we are going to explore two more layers of depth, giving them what they Want is a basic requirement. If they are expecting you to show them how you engage with specific consumers or what parameters you use for measurement, you need to tick these off as table stakes before you can take them further into what else you can do.

When our basic Wants are not met, we become hesitant, even resistant, to moving forward. It is worth thinking of delivering against their Wants as a way of earning their trust to move forward with you. If you can do this, they will be more willing to explore what else you can do, but if you can't meet their most basic expectations, why would they be open to hearing about what else you can do?

> **When our basic Wants are not met, we become hesitant, even resistant, to moving forward.**

When you are presenting in the absence of a brief – say, a proactive strategy or idea – then the Wants are the things you expect they would want to see in relation to the problem you have decided is worthy of solving. These will become a little more generic but are still worthy of your consideration because they will allow you to quickly connect your audience to your content, because these are things they are still expecting to see, even if they haven't told you as much.

Thinking about what they want from you, even in the absence of them telling you, enables you to connect your content to this basic expectation, and this keeps your audience engaged as you build the trust that you and your content have some relevance to them, which keeps the door open to begin to show what more you can do.

Spoken Needs

The next level after Wants is Spoken Needs. By the very nature of this level of needs becoming more personal and emotive, you won't see these written down anywhere. If you have a great relationship with the person in this position, these needs are what come up over a coffee when the rest of the team is not around.

It is the lean forward, the softly spoken moment in the conversation where they confide in you what they personally need, what help they need, and what will help them over and above solving the problem and delivering the requirements in the brief. This might relate to things they are judged on; where do they have to go over and above to stand out, get praise and be seen to be doing a 'good job' for the agency and the client? Where might they have gaps in knowledge or specific areas so they are going to need more from you than just what has been shared so far?

'Hey, I really need your help with … ' is what you'll hear them say.

If you don't have that kind of access or relationship, imagine that you did and, if you were having coffee with this person, what they would want to say to you to help them based on who they are, the experience they have and their personal motivations combined with their relationship to the problem. What do they need to be seen to be doing, what happens to them if they can't deliver on what is expected of them, and what impact is there to their relationship and the value they bring to others if they can't solve the problem?

Think about how they would say this with a level of vulnerability that you wouldn't see written down, and make sure to capture it in the first person to really feel their need.

All of these move from being just about solving the problem and what they want to see to the personal impact, the needs of the individual framed by their personal motivations that they would be prepared to share in a one-on-one conversation.

Here you are dancing on the line of rational to emotional. There is something tangible that needs to be delivered, an element of what is wanted, such as innovation in the response, but it now comes with a twist of personal implication, the spoken need of, 'I need to show that we are really pushing boundaries. I need to be seen as ... '.

This means more to them than an innovative idea; this is about helping them position themselves in the eyes of others. Do that for them and you deliver significantly more value than the innovative idea alone.

Unspoken Needs

Having established the Spoken Needs, you can now extend your thinking to the next level, but this time you won't be hearing about the Unspoken Needs over a coffee because, by their deeply personal nature, these needs are not spoken about.

You are now moving from the personal implications just beneath the surface to the underlying fears and insecurities that haunt our very core. We all have fears and insecurities, but we very rarely express them to anyone other than our closest friends or trusted confidants.

These Unspoken Needs live at the intersection of who they are (what they know and what they want) and the expectations they face (what others want and expect from them in their role). This intersection is where these two areas create a powerful set of highly charged emotions, such as the fear of failure, of letting people down, of not being good enough, of getting found out, and of not being seen as a driver. And, yes, these are all very negative and emotive, which is why they don't get spoken about but are incredibly powerful connection points.

And they exist in all of us; we all have fears and insecurities, whether they are real or not. In many instances, they are not; they are our perception of how others view us and our catastrophising the implications of not doing something as well as others might or might expect us to.

In more junior roles where you know their level of knowledge or experience in your area of expertise is not that advanced, Unspoken Needs can include the fear of getting found out for not knowing as much as they think they should and being exposed in front of a peer or client. But they are also too proud to admit this and don't seek to ask questions or explanations that would help them to learn and present your content with confidence. This is a major barrier to your success. If you know this exists in your audience, you have to find a way to give them what they need (the Unspoken Need in this case) or what you want, which is to stay in the game, won't be happening.

'Hey, in the appendix, I have created a ready reckoner of all the key terms and a quick explanation of each. I know you don't need this, but I thought it might help with some of the newer team members who have just started.' You know they *do* need it, but in your delivery you have given them what they need and made it comfortable for them at the same time. The emotional trust you build through this approach will elevate you and your response.

Following is an overview of how Wants help uncover Needs, and when Needs are understood, how the impact of these can be explored through thinking about the Unspoken Needs.

SOLVE FOR NEEDS. DON'T PLAY ON THEM.

The point of the Unspoken Needs is not to play on them but to solve them.

If you play on the Unspoken Need – let's say, playing on the fear of being found out by presenting in such a way as to heighten this by demonstrating how little the person knows about your technical capability in a certain area – this creates a stress response. As we discovered earlier, stress forms memories that are not in your interest; these are rigid and limited to being triggered by fixed associations that limit recall. None of that is good for your prospects with this audience, who also probably hate you right now. Another reason not to do this.

Suppose you can deliver your content in such a way that they can easily elevate their knowledge and confidently deliver your ideas without risk. You could include within your slides simple analogies that bring complex technical areas to life in an easy-to-explain way that anybody can remember. You might say these are aimed at a client who isn't as technical, while knowing you are doing this to help them present your ideas.

Now you are reducing the risk of them 'being found out', and you create greater relevance and trigger positive emotions. This encodes a stronger memory and positive associations for your content, which now cuts through the other presentations that are all rational and expected.

> **When you give them what they need, you are more likely to get back what you want – a real win–win.**

That is the shift you are looking for, the change in perspective from what you have to present to what they need from you. When you give them what they need, you are more likely to get back what you want – a real win–win.

Russell Pickering is the author of *Step into the Spotlight*, another great read if you wish to continue your learning after this book. He makes this point, which is a great summary for what we have just covered here:

When audiences hear you speak to their issues or concerns, empathise with them, be frustrated with them, hear their words articulated back to them, it builds trust and connection. Then, when you propose the solution or direction you wish to take them in, or the actions you want them to take, chances are your ability to persuade and motivate is improved. After all, why would I do anything you ask if I don't trust you or feel you understand me?

NEEDS

What matters to them

Wants

Written down

When they brief and work with media partners, what do they share in regard to their expectations from you to help them do their job well?

Functional elements such as:

- Bold ideas and innovation
- What you know about a specific audience or market
- Mandatory inclusions or exclusions; 'we want to see a timeline' or 'we want no more than two months of activity'
- Wanting validation or specific details on performance or measurement approaches

You have to give them **what they want** from you and have asked for in the brief.

Spoken Needs

Shared over coffee, not in writing

In their role, what are the things that they are judged on? Where do they have to go over and above to stand out, get praise and be seen to be doing a 'good job' for the agency and the client?

More emotive, personal measures such as:

Being seen to be pushing partners and boundaries, driving media firsts, getting additional value, and providing market insights 'off the record'.

'I really need you to help me out with this one...'

Solve for needs, don't play on them.

Unspoken Needs

Never talked about

What are their concerns and fears within their roles that don't get talked about but exist and can influence their decision-making?

The personal impact of not delivering on the spoken needs as well as their insecurities. Such as:

Not being seen as innovative and bold, the fear of letting down or losing a client, not being seen as a driver within the agency, not knowing something that impacts their status/reputation.

Solve for Unspoken Needs to form the **strongest emotional connections**.

Toolset #3: The change you see as possible

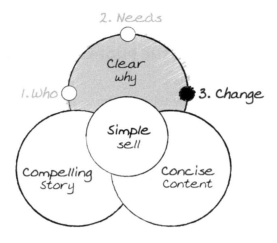

A presentation without a problem to solve is a presentation without a purpose.

The final set of tools in the Getting Clear toolbox is designed to help you define the change you see as being possible, defining how you can move your audience from the problem they have to a Better Place.

We buy things that solve our problems – if I don't have any problems, I don't need to spend money on solutions, or I won't spend very much money on something I don't think I need. Conversely, the bigger the problem, the more value there is in the solution.

In *Spin Selling*, Neil Rackham makes his view of solving problems very clear:

> *If you can't solve a problem for your customer, then there is no basis for a sale.*

My build on this is that the customer needs to be able to clearly see you are solving their problem, and for that to happen you need to know what it is you are solving.

When you are presenting, you want to make it as clear as possible that you are not just solving the problem your audience has. You are solving the biggest version of that problem, something I call Winter, which we will come to shortly.

NOT BEING CLEAR ON THE PROBLEM CREATES PROBLEMS

When you understand what the problem is, you can use it to help guide the development of your solutions and, importantly in this context, you can also use it to fine-tune the message, the narrative and even the slide headings to increase the audience's connection to your content.

But that means you need to be clear about what the problem is.

When a presentation is created without getting clear on the problem, it will invariably end up being all about you. What the idea is, how great the idea is, maybe how you came up with the idea and even why you love this particular idea.

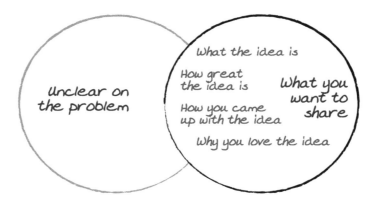

When this happens, not enough attention or thought is given to why any of this matters. It is left for the audience to determine exactly how this might benefit them; you hope they see the value, and see how your solutions solve their problems. When they don't or can't, you never hear from them again.

When needs don't align

When this is how a presentation comes together, it can mean that the audience and the presenter are coming at things from entirely the opposite ends of the spectrum.

One of the positions you have identified at your imaginary table is the person impacted by a problem: the Impacted.

Understanding what this person wants is very simple. They and anyone who is 'representing' them in your audience, such as the Connector, want to see this problem solved. What they are looking for from you and everyone else they are talking to is whether you have something to help them move from where they are right now to a Better Place. They are evaluating everything they see through this one lens: **what does this do for me?**

When you start with and build everything around what you have and what you want to sell, this can create a very unhelpful tension that can play out as a frustrated and agitated audience who are sitting through slide after slide thinking, *What has this got to do with us, and how does any of this help us or our client move forward?*

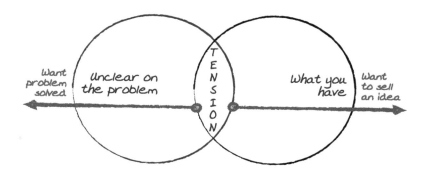

The problem is the gateway to your benefit

The purpose of understanding the problem in the context of the presentation is to shift the focus from what you have to what this does for them, your audience. That is what it means to be working from the problem perspective and not the 'what you have' perspective.

What this means is that everything in your presentation – your content, your story and your individual slides – needs to demonstrate clearly:

- how what you do helps them
- the change you see as possible.

Every slide that doesn't do this wastes time, attention and engagement compared to those that do or could. You need to connect your content to what the audience wants and is looking for; demonstrating how you solve their problem is giving them a reason to care.

> **You need to connect your content to what the audience wants and is looking for; demonstrating how you solve their problem is giving them a reason to care.**

And these benefits shouldn't be hidden or subtle – never assume the audience will get there themselves. Use the most prominent points on the slides, such as the headings, to land your most important points. Calling a slide 'The insight' is wasting the opportunity to highlight what your insight is.

Getting clear on the problem

So, if the problem is the gateway to being able to articulate and demonstrate your benefit, getting super clear on the problem you are solving is critical. You want to have a very simple statement to define your benefits, rather than a long list of buzzwords that lead you down multiple dead ends and rabbit holes and make structuring the content and story a lot more complicated.

Often the problem is either not well understood or is overly complex and wrapped up in strategic spin that can cloud what is happening and needs solving, leading you to structure your content around buzzwords rather than real tangible change and the benefit of this to the client. When you cut through this, it becomes easier to determine where your ideas connect and deliver these critical benefits.

I have a small confession here: I have been part of this issue. You see, people like me in fancy strategic roles like adding colour and pizzazz to the good old-fashioned problem statement. We must demonstrate how smart and strategic we are with our marketing jargon and fancy audience analysis Venn diagrams. Agencies and strategic consultants are paid a lot of money to understand clients' problems and identify specific issues and gaps within heavily researched and defined audiences. As a result, many slides are created to justify this expense. You could probably do in one or two slides what most strategists do in 10.

The brief might read something like this:

The brand seeks to foster a deeper and more meaningful connection with hipsters. A bond that forms a symbiotic relationship founded on mutual trust, with shared values and a sense of community.

Where the brand empowers the audience to embrace their freedom to challenge the cultural mainstream and express their individuality and uniqueness [insert Venn Diagram showing how unique the hipster is with little in common with the average folk of the same age profile].

The client seeks an innovative, out-of-the-box, media-first idea that brings this sense of connection and empowerment to the forefront of their minds and moves them to want to engage in non-traditional ways with the scope to create award-winning work with our tiny budget and tight turnaround.

Once you have cleared the small amount of strategic vomit from your throats, you need to work out the difference between what fuels your own strategic and creative process and the clarity you need to curate and deliver your content.

These are not the same thing, but all too often that distinction isn't made, and the brief bounces around like a checklist. Before you know it, you have a section on culture, individuality, empowerment and freedom but none of this is doing anything to demonstrate how you deliver the required change – you are just ticking off all the buzzwords in the brief.

The simpler you make the problem statement you are working with, the easier it will become to ascertain where you are solving the core problem and shine the spotlight on those benefits, which is what really matters. Here are the two things that are the key to the problem being useful in guiding the development of your presentation, tuning your narrative and creating specific slides that shine the spotlight on your benefits:

CHANGE

> **What's the simplest summary of the problem?**
>   − This must be free of jargon and fluff.
>   − Get all the rubbish out of the way to understand what is really going on in its simplest, most basic form.
>   − It can be helpful to think about how you would explain this problem to a grandparent; that will guide you to keep it really simple and free from marketing spin.

> **What help do they need?**
>   − Think about what they can't do that you might be able to help with.
>   − Then write a single sentence that captures the help they need.

The more help someone needs, the more value you have if you can provide that. Think about it: if I can reach certain customers using my CRM system and my data, I don't need any help, and while you might be able to reach that same audience, I don't see that as being of value. But if I can't reach hipsters because they don't see me as relevant, I need someone to help me, and that I will pay for.

The clearer you are on the core problem, the easier it becomes to both evaluate what you have to find your benefits and then bring these benefits to life in your content and on your slides without drifting off into the land of buzzwords and ending up with a convoluted and confusing narrative.

In the case of my hipster brief from earlier, the simplest version of the problem is: *This brand is struggling to connect with the hipster audience. Hipsters don't think it's a brand for them.*

And the help they need is: *To connect with the hipster audience in a way that doesn't alienate them.*

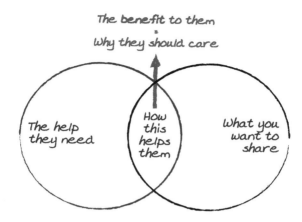

Getting down to this level of clarity is what you need to establish your benefits. Where what you have intersects with the help they need is where you are delivering a benefit to them. And because this is something they care about, it will connect them to your content and ideas; it is exactly what they are looking for.

Not only is this what you have to find, it is also what you have to put on show and spotlight. Make it as clear as you possibly can in the story you tell that this is how you are helping them move forward. You do not want them to miss a single benefit.

This might be as simple as a slide heading change that turns that slide from being about you (boring) to being about them – *bingo*, you are showing how you deliver value, having understood the problem and stripped it right back.

Try that simple change. Define the simplest version of the problem in a recent presentation. Find a slide in your deck and change the heading; keep the content the same but change the heading to make this about them – how this content is solving their problem – and the benefit you bring, not just what you have or do. And then, ask yourself which of these two versions is the most powerful at connecting your audience to your content.

This is about how you tune your content and your slides to demonstrate your value. Knowing this problem as you build your presentation will increase your connection through greater relevance and enhanced value.

When you can see the problem through the eyes of the audience, you will clearly see the benefits you can deliver for them.

But what if you could solve a bigger problem if the change you see as being possible is greater than that of your competitors?

> **When you can see the problem through the eyes of the audience, you will clearly see the benefits you can deliver for them.**

WINTER IS COMING

When a brief lands or there is an opportunity created where you are invited to present, it is hard to resist the temptation to go straight to solutions.

They have told you that they are struggling to connect their brand with a very specific audience, hipsters, a young, trend-setting lifestyle-orientated audience who don't follow the cultural mainstream. They see this brand as too traditional and outdated, but this audience represents a significant opportunity for growth if they can find a way to connect.

Your eyes light up. You know this audience well; you create content across several platforms specifically for them; you know you can be highly targeted in reaching this audience at scale; and you have a wealth of data both for insights and targeting. You can immediately see all the great ideas and products and can hardly contain yourself and start selling on the spot. You go straight from the problem to your potential solution, which I call the traditional approach.

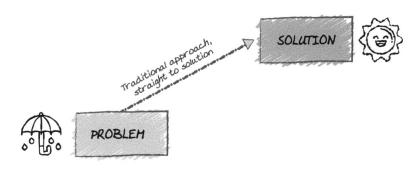

But wait.

What if, by doing this, you missed the chance to see how you could solve a bigger problem and demonstrate a greater change that could guide the construct of your content and your narrative? What if there was a way to apply your expertise to the problem your audience has and start your story from a completely different place to your competition, not just enhancing how you demonstrate your impact but also increasing the value in the journey you come up with? What if you could articulate how bad things could get for this client without you, based on what you know and your expertise in this area, painting a picture of the worst that can happen if they get this wrong or don't work with you?

When you go straight to the solution, you are in the comparison game, hoping your solution wins out based on features and what it does better than someone else, leaving yourself open to ending up in the price game, where there really isn't that much in it so the cheapest will win. Was all that work worth it just to end up in a price war?

You are starting from the same rational and known place as everyone else, running an equal race hoping to edge ahead at the very end when you drop the punchline.

Why not start somewhere different, from a place that evokes an emotional response right off the bat, forming that all-important connection, bringing the audience in to be part of your story, forming a bond around wanting to solve this bigger problem together, before you have even begun unpacking your solution?

Don't we want to solve their problem, not make it worse? Isn't it risky to start a presentation with a negative? Don't we want to be upbeat about what we bring and how we can save them?

Of course, and you will. In fact, you will solve the bigger problem and, in doing so, increase the impact, or at least the relative impact, of your solution. You are demonstrating your expertise and your knowledge of their problem through how you see it and what you know of how things can quickly get out of hand if not dealt with by the right partner.

In doing this, you are building an emotional connection to a new and more significant problem. Yes, you will have created it, but having taken your audience on the journey to get there, there is now this sense of being in this together. There is now a shared view of a bigger problem, one you have arrived at almost simultaneously as the story unfolded. As you pondered what was possible and how you could help, you saw there was this danger, this jeopardy that lay ahead for both of you. And now you are here and you both want the same thing, which is to get the hell out of here and away from this cold, dark Winter to a Better Place. The place you know you can and will take them to next. This is how you can form a story that brings them in from the outset and which feels like it's just for them – a story they want to see through to a resolution with you.

How powerful does that sound?

The job of Winter is to give you the biggest problem you can imagine and that you can solve. The idea behind calling this Winter was the phrase 'winter is coming' from the global phenomenon *Game of Thrones*. In this hit TV series, winter is the end of the world essentially. It is a bad view; in fact, the very worst view of what could happen.

Now, despite its origins, the Winter concept can be easily recalled without needing to remember this. Your starting point is always the current reality, the problem the Impacted person has that they want to solve.

Think of this as a grey day, overcast, with a little drizzle in the air. Not a beautiful day but not terrible either.

Now imagine taking this to a much worse place, taking this to Winter. This is a dark, cold time, heavy snow blocks roads, the sky is obscured by clouds, and it is cold and miserable. Somewhere you would like to escape and get to a Better Place.

Now imagine a hot summer day, beautiful blue skies and inviting warm water; after the cold of Winter, how good does it feel to imagine yourself there? That is the Better Place, the contrast that defines the change you see as being possible.

The purpose of Winter is to go back and imagine things getting worse before we go forward and get into solutions.

This is the opposite of where most people start – the inclination is to go from today, a little grey and chilly, to summer, the Better Place you see around the corner. That is, straight to the solution without a moment to pause and see what is at stake if you didn't solve their problem.

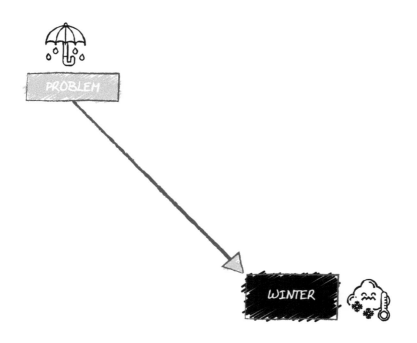

And this is a key point: what is at stake if you don't help to solve their problem? You are going to take that current reality and give it the Winter treatment; you are going to imagine how dark, cold, bleak and snowy it could become. You want to make things worse before you make them better.

What is at stake if you don't help to solve their problem?

The greater the change, the greater the value.

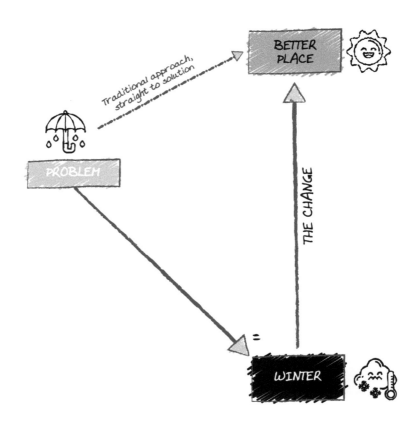

Perhaps at this point you are thinking, *But why bother?* You already know where you want to take them, and how you can solve their problem, so why go through this extra step? The simple answer is it will increase the apparent value of the solution you present, even if the solution is exactly the same. That is both the power and the point of Winter.

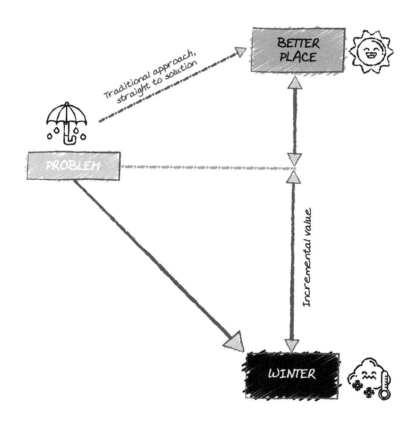

When you can demonstrate that there is a bigger change you see as being possible, when you can stop the worst that could happen without you from happening, you increase the perceived value of your solution. **That is both the point and the power of Winter.**

How do you Winterise a problem?

The good news is that most people find this very easy once they know the steps. We are inherently good at catastrophising, it seems. So put your catastrophising to good use and spin some Winter.

Let's step through the process.

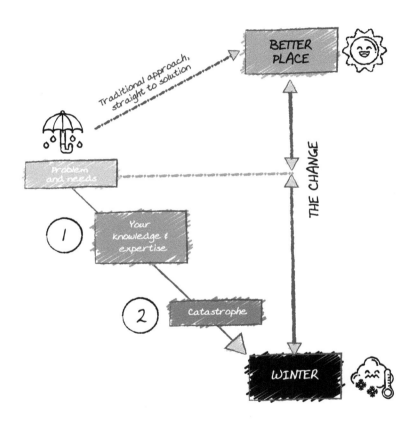

Problem + needs

Start by taking the problem your audience has, the one you have identified that the Impacted person wants solved, as do those representing them. Then consider the needs of your audience, both the spoken and unspoken. Which of these could be amplified or get worse if this problem isn't solved? For example, who might lose face, or could there be an impact on someone's status or reputation if this problem gets out of hand and things get worse?

Apply your knowledge and expertise

What expertise do you have in relation to the help you have defined they need when you simplify the problem? For instance, with the earlier example of the brand that needs help to connect in a way that doesn't alienate hipsters, what expertise do you have in attracting, growing or building a relationship with this audience, the hipsters? What do you know about them? How hard are they to reach? How difficult are they to engage? How fickle are they when it comes to messages, content or advertising? How have you seen attempts to connect with the audience go wrong in the past?

If it is related to a technical capability that is missing, becoming outdated or not well understood, what are the implications of this remaining so? What happens to clients who don't overcome these challenges? What happens when the status quo is maintained in a rapidly advancing world? What happens when technology becomes outdated?

These are the things to consider at this stage of Winterising the problem.

There is one important distinction to the application of your expertise. You are applying what you know about the problem based on your area of expertise; this will probably revolve around your knowledge of your audience and how they interact with your products or services. You might be an expert in entertainment, content consumption, digital behaviour, technology usage – this is all incredibly valuable. You should avoid trying to be an expert in your client's business; it is unlikely you will know the inner workings of finance, aviation, travel, government or automotive sectors to the same extent as your client. They spend millions on research and live and breathe their sector every day. Apply the expertise you bring to the problem from what you know about what you do. This is extremely valuable, positions your expertise, and can't easily be challenged or refuted.

CHANGE

Catastrophe

What happens without you?

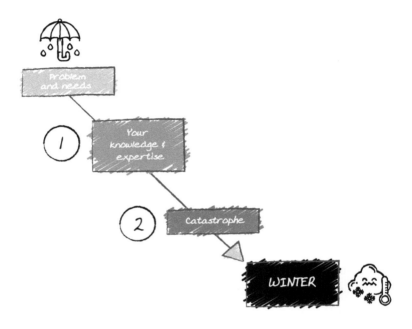

What could you foresee happening based on your knowledge and expertise in this area?

You now want to continue this line of thinking. Continue to imagine how this problem can escalate without you, the implications of what you know and how this specific problem and these needs spiral into a cold, dark place if not resolved.

Here is where a little catastrophising allows you to imagine things getting much worse and creates a much bigger problem to solve. You are, in essence, creating a continuum from problem to Winter, and you can decide how far down you want to go in each situation. I call that the 'continuum of darkness'.

In the case of my hipster example, this is how I would play this out:

Hmm, hipsters are a tough audience to engage with. I mean, they generally don't like advertising. They don't like brands that preach to them or run overt promotions or tactics to get their attention.

They like to feel like they have discovered brands that no-one else knows about.

You have to work to earn their trust. And they don't trust brands, so you have to think like them, understand them and work on connecting with them from the inside out.

We have seen this go badly wrong. I mean, like brands being completely rejected when they have tried to win them over and got it all wrong.

Rejection. That feels bad, right? Yep, that is Winter.

Without someone who can build a trusting relationship and who understands this audience, there is a risk of alienating them. That is what is at stake without your solution – assuming, of course, you know this and can build the required trust.

This is what it looks like to move down the continuum of darkness.

Defining the change from Winter to a Better Place, the change that you see as being possible, comes before the benefit you have or how you solve their problem.

Winter is not about explaining the benefits of your solution; it is the exact opposite, explaining what happens when your solution doesn't exist.

This is your unique perspective. It is the value you bring to solving this problem that should not go to waste by simply going straight to the solution without laying out what you know and the impact of this knowledge not being applied. Failing to follow your guidance will leave the audience languishing in Winter. As you unpack this, they will see the value in what you bring even though you have yet to talk about what you do or your strategies, ideas or solution.

Paint a picture of the dark, cold days ahead.

Winter is a summary of what you can imagine happening, written as a short statement.

In this case: *there is a risk of being rejected by hipsters.*

Don't Winterise your own problems

The problem has to be the problem they, your audience, has, such as reaching and connecting with a specific audience, confidence in digital measurement or the need for greater marketing efficiency.

This should not be a problem you have. If clients are not spending enough with you, this is your problem, not theirs. If you apply Winter to this, you have made your own problem worse. Don't do that. Winterise their problem.

When you solve the bigger problem for them, the more you increase the emotional appeal and, therefore, the value of the story and the content that delivers this.

Is this a slide? Yes, almost certainly.

The next question I get is should I make a slide about Winter?

When you come to look at the story structure in the chapter on creating a compelling story, you will see the importance I place on *establishing* the basis for your presentation, the starting point of your story. Your work to establish a powerful and relevant Winter that you are comfortable delivering is by far the most effective way to do this.

For instance, a slide with 'a fine line between rejection and connection' could work well as a heading in my hipster presentation. Or you can have a slide on their problem and then a voiceover saying how this could escalate to Winter based on your experience.

What I typically find is when people start to work with Winterising problems they are most comfortable voicing this over, but as they see the impact of this and their confidence grows with how to play with it and apply it across the different problems and audiences they work with, it then starts to become a slide at the beginning of the presentation and often one they really enjoy presenting!

As you may have noticed, I call the problem to Winter journey the continuum of darkness, and that is because you get to choose how far you take Winter based on your knowledge of your audience and your confidence in delivering this in slide or voiceover form. You might initially create slides with a mild Winter and play with adding a bit more freeze in your narrative. You need to be both comfortable and confident in what you are delivering, so this will always be a judgement call for you to make on each occasion.

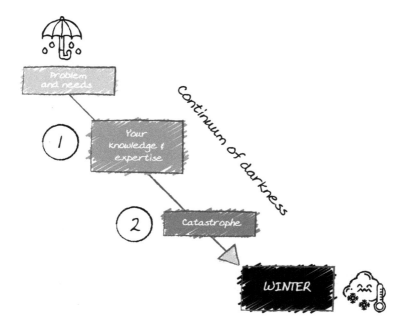

The change

The final part of Winter is to establish the change from Winter to a Better Place. This is a critical step because you can't leave your audience in Winter; you created it, and now you need to determine what the contrast looks like and what is possible to get them out of there.

Let's be very clear; it is bad for business to leave your audience frozen in Winter. You take them there with the single-minded goal of leaving there as quickly as possible and getting to a Better Place.

Once you have defined this contrast, it will be clear to you what this presentation is about and how you can begin to structure your content to take the audience from the Winter you have defined to your Better Place, the change that this presentation will deliver.

How to go about this

Having established the dark and cold Winter and describing how bad things could get, you can now use this to fuel how you can describe the Better Place you can see.

What is the contrast to Winter? What is the Summer to the Winter you have created?

This is not how you will affect that change, nor all the details of your solution to overcome their problem, but your vision for what is possible by working with you.

In very simple terms, if we call Winter point A, Summer is point B, the Better Place you can see as being possible, and the impact of working with you. Your change is to go from A to B.

The point of your presentation is to bring to life this change, to unpack how you do that, the steps you take, the things you have, and all the elements of the how. The change is designed to help you create that story and the navigation to take the audience on that journey with you.

If Winter is being rejected by hipsters who feel targeted by this brand, your view of the contrast of summer, the place you believe your solution can take your audience to, is that hipsters are discovering the brand and creating a sense of belonging and ownership. They feel they have found this brand by chance, and it now belongs to them and their hipster brothers and sisters and no-one else.

From A to B, and the 'so what?' is the B, the Better Place.

A: Being rejected by hipsters who feel targeted by this brand.

B: Hipsters discover the brand.

That's it.

Not how you will do this, no explanation of what you will do, just what you believe is possible as the alternative to Winter.

Done well, this becomes a very powerful and incredibly versatile strategic lever.

What does the Winter of this book look like? Go back and read pages 11 and 12 again. Here you will see Winter in action as I set up the change that I see as being possible for you. That is the Winter for this book.

On the following page is the Winter worksheet. A copy of this can also be downloaded here: www.davidfish.com.au/downloads/wp.

Winter and the change worksheet

What problem have you identified that the Impacted person wants to solve? Then consider the needs of your audience. Which of these could be amplified or made worse if this problem isn't solved? Who might lose face? Could there be an impact on someone's status or reputation if this problem gets out of hand and things get worse?	**Problem and needs**
What expertise do you have in relation to the help that you have defined they need when you simplify the problem? What do you know about this topic? What data, research and experience can you apply?	**Knowledge and expertise**
What happens without you? Imagine how this problem can escalate, the implications of what you know, and how this specific problem and these needs spiral into a cold, dark place if not resolved. Paint a picture of what could be at stake and how bad things can get. What do you know or foresee happening if their problem isn't solved, gets worse or is approached in the wrong way?	**Catastrophise**

CHANGE

Winter (A)

Write a simple summary of how bad things could get.

The contrast to define the change (B)

What is the contrast to Winter? What is the Summer to the Winter you have created?

In very simple terms, if we call Winter point A, then Summer is point B, the Better Place you can see as being possible, the impact of working with you.

Your change is to go from A to B.

Once you have defined this contrast, it will be clear what this presentation is about and how you can begin to structure your content to take the audience from the Winter you have defined to your Better Place, the change this presentation will deliver.

This is different from how you will affect that change. It is not all of the details of your solution to overcome their problem, but your vision for what is possible by working with you.

The point of your presentation is to bring to life this change, to unpack how you do that, the steps you take, the things you have, and all the elements of how you will do this. The change is designed to help you create that story and the navigation to take the audience on that journey.

Getting Clear conclusion

In this chapter on Getting Clear, we have covered what it means to be:

► clear on who matters to you
► clear on what matters to them
► clear on what is possible, the problem you are solving for them and how to define the biggest change to increase your value.

While this is certainly a starting point, the power of undertaking this work is so much more than a foundation; these are game-changing tools. If you do nothing more than apply these, your presentations will improve, as will your confidence as a presenter.

By applying this thinking, you will:

► increase your confidence in the value you can deliver for your audience
► increase your ability to bring your audience into your story with relevance and a strong and lasting emotional connection
► build the confidence to solve the bigger problem, one that also elevates your solution and its value above your competition.

The key to this is to stop leading with what you have and make the shift to starting every presentation with an audience in mind. Pause for a moment to think about them, to feel what it is like to be them in their role and to imagine how much worse their problem could become without you.

When you get clear on who and why you are creating this presentation, it acts like an anchor on a boat. It stops you drifting off and hitting the rocks when the going gets rough. When everyone has a suggestion for what should be included and what you should present, and you are trying to keep control, filter and organise your content, you can go back to who this is for, what they need and the change you see as being possible. This will anchor your presentation right from the outset.

When you get clear on who and why you are creating this presentation, it acts like an anchor on a boat.

When you use these three tools effectively, it will increase the confidence you have in the value of your message to your audience.

To help you with this important set of tools and what they uncover for you, here is a simple checklist that can capture everything you need as you work through developing your presentation from here.

In the next chapter, you will see how this work helps with shaping content and making it easier for you to present and easier for your audience to recall. And then how it sets up the story arc and enables you to develop a compelling story with ease and elegance, creating a narrative that draws your audience in from the very start and has them following along as you navigate through to your powerful resolution.

Checklist: Getting clear on why this presentation exists

CLEAR

The roles that matter, your audience is:	Simple problem statement:	The benefits we have are:
Connector:		
Influencers:		
Impacted:		
They want:	Winter is coming:	
Their needs are:	The change we see as possible is:	

TOOLBOX 2:
CONCISE CONTENT

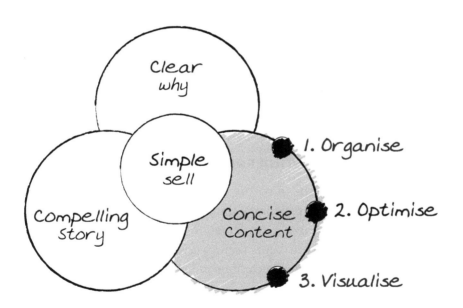

AVOIDING OVERWHELMING AND CONFUSING CONTENT

Slide content is the lifeblood of a sales presentation, unlike a keynote presentation where you are the star and the slides are the support act. In a presentation that delivers strategies, ideas and solutions to technical problems, you require the audience to understand what you have presented and have the confidence and the content to present to others without you there. That means there needs to be more than just an image and a word on a slide. I love clean and powerful slides like this, but they don't work in this context.

You have to strike a balance between having too little content to support your point and too much that overwhelms and confuses – sometimes, both you and the audience! And the latter is the most common problem in most organisations; that is expecting the audience to drink in content fired at them through a firehose.

Slide content is the lifeblood of a sales presentation, unlike a keynote presentation where you are the star and the slides are the support act.

COMPLEXITY ISN'T YOUR FRIEND

Dan Sullivan coined the term 'the Ceiling of Complexity™', and his work goes some way to explaining the underlying issue that sits behind the overburden of content in presentations. He discusses the idea that as you expand what you have, there is a subtle pressure to increase your responsibilities and expectations in line with this expansion.

Essentially as you create more, there is an expectation of using everything you have created. Eventually, this expectation adds a layer of complexity that becomes a ceiling on any further progress. You have so much that even you become stuck without a clear way forward.

Here's how I see this playing out in presentations

You start with feeling like you don't have enough of something; not enough products to sell, not enough proof points, not enough ideas – 'What if they don't like that one? We should cover a couple of bases with a few more ideas' – even insufficient slides to make a valid argument or look like you have really thought this through – 'We can't present a $1 million solution on just one slide ... can we?'

This then leads to expansion, which starts out as a positive. You go into creator and hunter mode, resolving this feeling by creating and hunting for more and more content to make it look like you are delivering value and depth. The content bank builds as you collect ideas and slides to fill what might have been a void and is now a growing mountain.

The problem is that as you expand what you have, there is this silent expectation that you have to keep everything you have found. This can even be the expectations of others: 'We created that for you, and we expect to see it presented. You know how long we worked on that.'

There is an expectation you will include *everything*, squeeze in every product's poof point, every idea, however relevant or not – and you simply must present every single slide in the deck.

Ever felt the expectation to include more just because it was there? This is when you hit the ceiling of complexity. Your expansion has become your limitation. In my experience, this is the point at which you are significantly diminishing your value and even becoming hard to buy. Without a proper framework to guide you, the content and organisation of your presentation are quickly getting out of control and limiting your ability to get your message across. That is the ceiling of complexity as it relates to your content.

That determination to fulfil against your self-imposed expectations and those of others has been left unchecked. And now, it is getting harder to win and convert business.

This shows up as:

- I hope we don't overwhelm them with all of our content, our acronyms and jargon.
- I hope they can see the bigger idea in all of the stuff we have.
- I hope they can find what they need to present our ideas.

This is where this chapter and the exercises coming up become critical. You have to be able to determine how to organise, optimise and visualise your content. What is critical is how you control the flow of information and create a logical narrative and navigation to keep your audience engaged and following along. As well as what should be left out!

Buying the flour

I sat on a review panel for a major client looking at a range of existing and new technology partners. It was a significant contract, and while the client was integral to the decision, I was running the agency that would hold the contract, so we all had a keen interest in what was being presented and offered.

It was a mixed bag of presentations. There was, without question, a high degree of complexity to the solutions being presented and some technical knowledge was required to get beyond the surface sizzle, which, if you were not careful, could draw you in without really knowing what was being offered. On the other hand, there was a point at which further unpacking the system's inner working was not required. The point had been made; there was enough to understand what made this work and why it was different. The next level and beyond created unnecessary questions driven by an increasing uneasiness as the technical jargon drowned even the most competent in the room.

Questions are both a sign of interest and a sign of gaps in understanding. When the questions stop, you may have answered everything or the audience may have given up trying to close the gap and switched off because they are overwhelmed. This was certainly the case on this occasion.

In one particular presentation, every single ingredient was on show, unpacked almost to the code that ran the software. Each was explained with an excruciatingly detailed level of technical information. This was slow, painful and unnecessary.

> **Questions are both a sign of interest and a sign of gaps in understanding.**

Then the mood in the room changed. The client had seen something, a widget, that caught their eye. They understood what this widget did, they were excited and keen to learn more. The presenter was quick to point out that this was just one part of a much bigger solution. But, alas, the game was already over for them. There was no recovery from the shiny widget the client had their eye on for the next 30 minutes (15 minutes more than their allotted time). The client hammered them with questions about this one tiny element they wanted. Try as they might, with their team now rallying around their drowning presenter, they could not recover.

The meeting ended with the client intent on buying something akin to 1% of the main idea.

What caught their eye wasn't what they really wanted from their partner or, indeed, what they needed, but everything else, including the broader solution, was falling into the too-hard basket. What had been presented was way too detailed and technical, and it was reliant on the client piecing everything together like Lego bricks strewn across the floor. It needed the client to have the vision of what could be possible. When they saw the one brick they needed to finish a project, a brick they recognised, they jumped at it. Left strewn all around were the hundreds of other pieces that together could be used to make something quite incredible, but they were left for the outgoing presenters to sweep up and take away, never to be seen again.

Coming up in this toolbox are three toolsets to enable you to:

▶ **Organise** all of your content by combining elements to increase their utility and establish the higher level offering, and create an order that brings logic to how you unpack the content, making it easier to follow, easier to explain and easier for your audience to review and share.

▶ **Optimise** the flow of information to enhance the delivery of the main points. Laddering up to establish what matters most, and the point of this, makes it easy to recall the key points for you and them and find that content within the presentation a day, a week or a month later.

▶ **Visualise** how you deliver the change on a page and be ready to present anywhere at any time with a single slide. *If you can draw it, you can explain it to anyone.* The goal of this toolset is to be able to create a presentation on a page – the Hero Slide, as I call it.

CONCISE

Toolset #1: Organised content

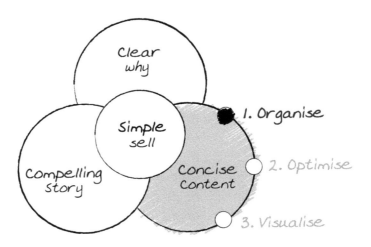

Selling the dish not the ingredients.

The starting point for getting organised is that not everything you have is of equal value, not everything needs to be included or presented to the level of detail you have right now, and you need some order to how this content is brought together and then unfolds.

Without this, you run the real risk of overwhelming the audience with too much of everything. You know, if you went to a fast-food restaurant and ate everything on the menu, you would feel a little sick afterwards. Just because it is there doesn't mean you must have it all right now.

When you have too much content, too much detail and too much information for them to take in and recall, your audience can feel a little sick too. Which in presentation language means overwhelmed and confused. I don't know about you, but I can't recall the last time I made a decision to move forward with something important when I was overwhelmed and confused.

And it gets worse. There is very little chance that your audience will later present something where the level of detail exceeds their level of knowledge and comfort. The risk of being called out, of being embarrassed by not being to explain something when questioned by a peer or boss, means they will shy away from presenting anything you have made look complicated or with more detail than they are comfortable with.

Nobody will ever present something they don't understand

If you organise your content from a high-level concept down into the detail, they can take the level they are most comfortable with and make it their own without fear of getting lost in detail, keeping your solutions alive and you still in the game.

ORGANISE

Nobody will ever present something they don't understand

TURNING INGREDIENTS INTO A DISH

For this set of exercises to organise your content, I want you to start by thinking about your available content as food. To be more specific, as the raw ingredients, the most basic and typically the largest volume of things you could put out into the world.

Those ingredients might be certain types of ad units, a range of different products you sell or the different elements of a solution. All of the elements you typically lay out on your slides.

Now you could present everything as it is and, in so many instances, people do. They put all of the raw ingredients out on show for the audience to pick at like a seagull picking at some chips on the ground, and they hope they can see the bigger idea is all of the stuff they have on display. This not only confuses and overwhelms the audience, but also devalues your products, ideas and solutions, and this is what we want to avoid.

In this toolset you will work through how to:

1. combine to increase value
2. group to increase utility
3. order to make it easier to present and recall.

Step 1: Combine

The first step is to look at all of your ingredients and determine what you can bring together to create something that will **increase the value for your audience** based on their wants and needs.

Following my analogy, let's say I have an audience who needs breakfast to get their day going; they are busy and want something ready to eat that is tasty and a little bit indulgent but easy to grab and go. I have some flour, eggs, maple syrup and lemon, which on their own are not that useful for my busy executives running to their first meeting of the day. By presenting them with these raw ingredients, I am not exactly meeting their needs or their wants. They would quite rightly see very little value in what I have to offer them at this point.

Last time you were rushing to a meeting and wanted a quick snack, how useful were flour and eggs?

If I combine all of these ingredients, I can increase the value of what I have relative to the needs of my audience quite significantly when I offer them pancakes with a drizzle of maple syrup and a squeeze of lemon.

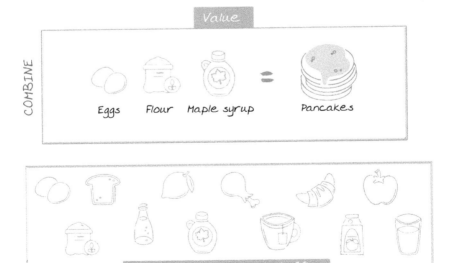

This one simple step has taken me from offering next to no value, with a collection of 'stuff' that probably won't be remembered by my audience, to not only meeting their needs but also doing so with something that is easier for them to recall and tell others about.

Which would you prefer to have on a busy morning, and which would you pay more for? The pancakes with a drizzle of maple syrup or the flour and the eggs?

In my workshops, I do this very exercise but with real ingredients and I ask one hungry participant how much they would pay for the raw ingredients versus the beautiful warm and fluffy pancakes. On one occasion, I was offered $2 for the ingredients and $21 for the pancakes with a drizzle of maple syrup. That is a great illustration of the value of creating a dish if ever I saw one.

This first step is about looking across all your raw ingredients and seeing what you can combine to make it more desirable for your audience. You are adding two or more things together to create one new item, something with a higher order value than the individual pieces on their own.

One trap here is to think you need to create new products when that isn't part of your role; someone else in the business oversees products. This is actually about packaging what you have, the three or four products strewn across the one slide, bringing them together and giving them a new heading, which allows you to combine them into one or maybe two tasty dishes. This simple step takes your content up one level and helps you start to control the narrative.

The second thing that concerns people at this stage is 'they are losing things' and 'stuff is being taken away'. Yes, and no. Yes, in so much as that is the point. We want to take things away from view to make what we highlight more impactful. However, everything you started with is still there; it is just rolled up into something more useful as a starting point. This means that if you need to unpack this, you can.

If someone asks me how I make my delicious pancakes and what goes into them, *then* I can talk about the flour, eggs and Canadian Maple Syrup that I use, but I don't start there; I only go there if the audience wants and needs this level of detail. Those ingredients are never lost; they are just one level out of view because I want the attention on what they make and the value of that to my audience, and not on the basic ingredients used to get there.

ORGANISE

Market stalls don't make as much as restaurants that sell tasty dishes. You don't want to be a market stall.

And this is a critical point; everything we are working on from this point is about **how _you_ control the flow of information to your audience**. You are moving away from putting everything on show and hoping for the best to curating your content and then your narrative and story to guide them, to draw their attention to what you want them to see and recall, making it easier to find the key points and the slides they need to present your content without you.

Market stalls don't make as much as restaurants that sell tasty dishes. You don't want to be a market stall.

Step 2: Group

Having worked through and combined your raw ingredients, you should now have a number of new dishes, such as the pancakes we just created, as well as the other pieces of content you are happy are already at the right level to demonstrate their value to your audience.

The next step is to look for the themes within your content to see how you could create groups of content with similar or related items. The purpose of this is to begin to leverage logic to make it easier to organise your content into a flowing story, and to increase the ease with which you can recall and present each element and your audience can follow along. This is about creating greater utility **for you** and **your audience**.

If I stick with the food analogy and think about the different dishes I could have created by combining ingredients, I can think about a number of themes, such as:

▶ small, medium and large dishes
▶ carbs, calorie and vitamin values
▶ dishes you would have as snacks, dinners and breakfast
▶ dishes for family meals, on-the-go, healthy and as a side dish.

You can see that quite quickly you can come up with a number of themes that might bring everything together into a smaller number of groups organised by a connecting theme.

You want to pick a theme that creates the most logical groups for the content you have and the audience's problem you are solving. You are not trying to be clever; in fact, just the opposite. You want to find the most natural, most obvious, most logical groups, because these are the ones that will be the easiest for everyone to grasp quickly and form a mental picture around.

Let's take meal occasions. Everyone knows what these are. I don't have to establish when breakfast happens, or that lunch is in the middle of the day, or justify or explain the types of foods people usually have on each occasion.

ORGANISE

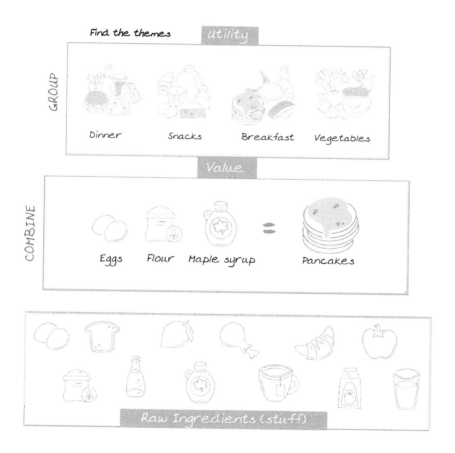

This is all known and well understood, which creates some immediate short cuts for my content. Just by saying I have something that might be of interest to you at breakfast, you have a mental picture of where this fits in your world and the relevance to your needs.

If I said I would love to come and present my flour and water solution to your hunger problem, what image does that create, and how easy is it for the audience to see where I might be of use to them?

The groups are the first level of mental short cuts that you will keep refining to make it easier to unpack your content and make it stick.

When I look across my dishes, I can see I can group what I have into dinner, snacks and breakfast, and I also have a separate group of vegetables.

What you are looking to do as you work through which groups work best to bring your content together is to think about these as sections of your presentation and whether having these groups will help you take the audience from the problem to the Better Place you see as being possible after navigating through your solution to land this change.

In my example, I have the vegetable group to one side. This creates an important opportunity to check my content and decide whether this should be left out completely. It doesn't fit within the best version of my narrative from the problem to the change I see as possible. Maybe this content should be part of the other groups, and I missed this the first time around and can now incorporate them back into my three other groups. Or it could be a sign that the groups and themes I have chosen are not the right ones.

> **The purpose of grouping is to bring your content (dishes) together through the natural themes that exist so you end up with three to six groups.**

If the vegetable dish is one of my best pieces of content to show the audience how I am solving their problem and moving them forward and, therefore, must be included, and I can't find a way to incorporate this into the groups I have, then my groups are not the right ones. Maybe the themes of family meals, on-the-go, healthy and side dishes would work better.

The purpose of grouping is to bring your content (dishes) together through the natural themes that exist so you end up with three to six groups.

Why three to six? If the average presentation is delivered in a one-hour window, three to six sections are the optimum number. Fewer than three and you run the risk of not punctuating your content enough into sections to create a flow to the navigation that makes it easier to consume, follow and find content later.

More than six and these sections become very light on the detail, or you have too much content for the time you have to present, with questions. You have not combined and grouped effectively enough to manage the content you have.

So, the question you are asking yourself as you work through this is this: what are the three to six groups organised by a common theme that will help you navigate from the problem to your Better Place through the change you see as being possible?

Depending on the amount of content you have (the number of dishes you have come up with), there are a couple of practical ways to find themes and create groups.

You can draw six boxes on a sheet of paper, or use sticky notes (which is my preferred option for a big presentation with lots of content). You are organising your content to see what themes connect different items and create a group:

- How many items fit into each group? Is it balanced or are there two large groups and two shallow ones? You want your groups to have a semblance of balance.
- What other groups would work alongside this?
- Is there a logic to these groupings, or do they feel a bit forced?
- Does this give you three to six groups that contain the key elements of your content?
- How much is left out or hard to make fit? Is that a problem, or helpful to refine your content down?
- Are these groups known to your audience? Breakfast and lunch are universally understood, whereas diets such as Paleo and keto could be known to you but not universally understood by your audience, requiring either an explanation or risking confusion.

Here are a few common themes you could use as thought starters, but there are literally hundreds, so don't be constrained by these:

▶ establish, create, share, distribute
▶ now, next, future
▶ awareness, education, consideration, action, review
▶ who, what, when, where
▶ why, how, what, so what
▶ inform, excite, engage, share
▶ frame, awareness, reminders, triggers
▶ mass, targeted, personalised, one to one
▶ awareness, consideration, conversion
▶ discovery, interest, appraisal, review.

You get the idea. Within your content there will be some natural themes. Your goal is to find the ones that allow you to create three to six balanced groups that bring your content together in a more organised and logical way.

The differences between Combine and Group are:

▶ With Combine, you are creating **something new** from two or more things. What you create is more important than the ingredients that go into it. The dish sits above the ingredients.
▶ With a Group, you are **keeping what you have** (not making anything new) but looking to bring things together based on **themes that unite them.**

Step 3: Order

The final step is a very simple one.

You should have formed three to six groups by this stage; now, you want to apply one final piece of logic to these and determine the order in which they should be organised. What you are looking to establish is this:

▶ What determines their natural order? Does one have to occur before another? Or do they build one on top of the other?
▶ Is there an obvious relationship between these groups?

The relationship between breakfast, snacks and dinner is time. They are sequenced by the time of day, so that sets the order. It is logical to present my content about breakfast before my snack content, which comes before my dinner content, because this is the logical order for my audience to follow.

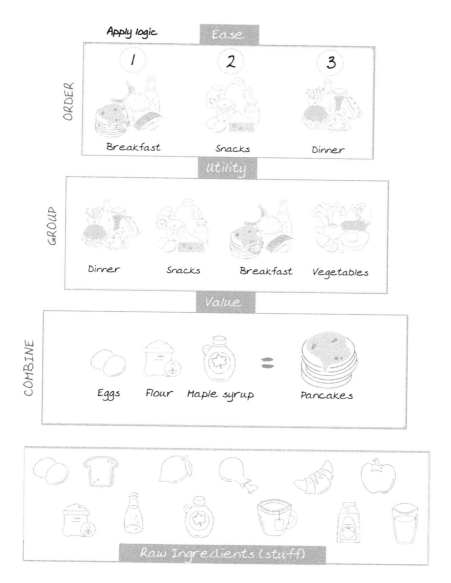

ORGANISE

Suppose I had grouped content by marketing funnel themes and had Appraisal, Interest and Discovery as my three content groups. The most logical order is Discovery, Interest and then Appraisal, which becomes the order of my groups.

There are two reference points. The first is the most logical flow, and the second is the problem you are solving and how the order of your content moves your audience from the problem through the change you see as possible to the Better Place.

Your audience will see this content for the first time when you present it. Leveraging a logical flow helps them to anticipate what might be next, to catch up quickly if they fall behind and to find what they need when they come back to your content in days, weeks or months. If I were to present Dinner, Breakfast and then Lunch, how does that feel?

The organisation of your content in this way, combining, grouping and establishing the order, will take you from a collection of stuff that you run the risk of presenting like a market stall to enabling you to lay out your content with strategic intent, taking your audience on a logical flowing journey from their problem to your solution with nothing to get in the way or distract them. In doing this, we have already gone from having 20-plus pieces of content (ingredients) that would have been impossible to overview and potentially hard to present trying to remember what was coming next, to summarising this down to my three groups of Breakfast, Snacks and Dinner in the order in which we will probably present them.

If you had to right now, you could explain this to someone else who would easily be able to recall what is in your presentation in a few days.

The two most common objections I get as we work through this are:

▶ Haven't I lost some things we spent time creating?

▶ What if I need some of the detail to explain things further?

What you have achieved is an understanding of what matters most. Your investment into expansion is fine-tuned, enabling you to move straight to the problem and resolution conversation. This will unlock more value for you and for your customers than any shopping list ever will.

However, everything you started with is still there; it is just organised, refined and ordered. If you need to drop down a level and explain something further, you can. You can even include this level of content in your presentation if you really have to, knowing you intend to skip this slide but it is there if you need it.

Everything we do in this chapter is about giving you more control over how to lay out and present your content – what comes first and how far you intend to go, and how far you can go. When you organise in this way, you will no longer be trapped by linear slides unfolding in front of a perplexed and frustrated audience with no way out for you. You can adapt and expand as you determine it is needed.

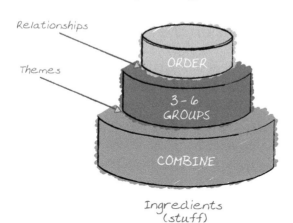

Organising Content

ORGANISE

Toolset #2: Optimise

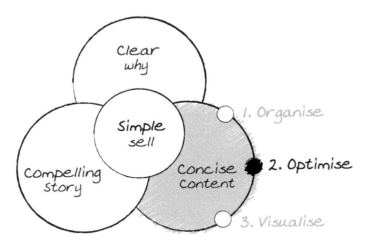

Take control of what it means and when they see it.

Having organised your content into groups and established the order based on the relationships, you can now go one step further by laddering up to enhance the content delivery within each group. The goal is to be able to explain what each group represents in a summary form, from a phrase that establishes the essence of what that group represents through the main point and down into the details.

Why do this? You already have three to six groups, so why go through these extra steps to optimise the groups this way?

Well, there are quite a few benefits to this:

► It is helpful to you to establish what each group contains, because this will help you remember what content goes in there and what this group represents. As your final content comes together, you can quickly decide what slides go where and avoid excess and inappropriate content creeping in that can dilute and pollute the clarity of the work you have done to organise your content logically and inform the flow of your story.

- By being able to explain the main message of each group, it will be easier to organise the content within the group to expand and bring this message to life, providing a final level of the hierarchy. What information must you get across to the audience, and what is support or secondary or could be dropped if you have too much content?

- It will be easier to form the overall narrative and then lay out the content on slides to ensure the most important information lands first and that you retain the logical flow, having worked through this.

- This is your first opportunity to move from functional explanations, 'what this is', to reframe this around why the audience should care, describing what it does for them and the benefit it brings. In doing so, you are giving them a greater reason to pay attention even before you unpack the content in this section.

- As you learn to master creating shorter, punchier and more descriptive statements to establish what each group is about, you will find that this aids your recall of what this is about, making it easier to present but also for your audience to quickly get a sense of what is coming up, navigating your content with ease as you deliver it and also, importantly, enabling them to find key pieces of content within the presentation a day, a week or a month later. This is a key skill of the Strategic Storyteller and one worth spending the time to develop.

We remember catchphrases, analogies and metaphors much more easily than jargon and technical terms, and certainly much more readily than stats and figures.

We remember catchphrases, analogies and metaphors much more easily than jargon and technical terms, and certainly much more readily than stats and figures. When done well, establishing what each group is about creates a visual signpost to this content. Optimising your content in this way will allow you to control the flow of information, starting with the most important and layering down into more detail where it is needed or called for.

Think of this like a ladder, with each rung getting narrower as you move closer to establishing the essence of what this is all about, using fewer and fewer words to become as concise as possible.

Far too often I see the exact opposite; presentations start with all the detail on display and try to bring this together over time, each slide building towards some magical crescendo where the presenters hope it all makes sense. There is a misconception they should not give away the ending but sustain excitement with this supposedly clever reveal.

The problem is that by the time you reach the reveal, the audience can be completely lost and unable to make the expected connection or any connection at all, and just sees a lot of detail that they find hard to know what to do with it.

Tell them what this is about, set up what is coming next and then work down into the detail as needed, stepping through what you have outlined is coming and then bringing it all back together again.

A great way to remember this is to think about how a book is structured.

The book title **establishes** what this is all about in a few exciting words that draw you in: Winning Presentations.

It gives you enough information to establish if this is of interest to you and makes it easy to recall what this particular book is about relative to all the others on your bookshelf.

Then comes the subtitle, which **explains** the main message to provide more meaning for the audience: why being a good presenter is often not enough and why the best ideas don't always win.

If this interests you, that is what this book will cover.

Then the book is structured to expand on this with enough detail to deliver against this.

So, for each of your groups, you can imagine them as little books of content; what goes on the front cover of each is what you want to work out to optimise how you control the flow of information.

How to optimise your content

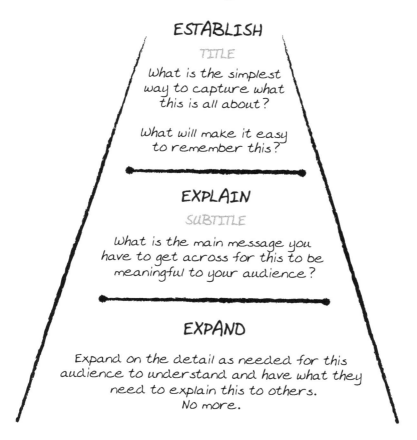

ESTABLISH

TITLE

What is the simplest way to capture what this is all about?

What will make it easy to remember this?

EXPLAIN

SUBTITLE

What is the main message you have to get across for this to be meaningful to your audience?

EXPAND

Expand on the detail as needed for this audience to understand and have what they need to explain this to others.
No more.

I can establish Breakfast under the title Power Up with an explanation (subtitle) of *the meal that gets you going.*

Snacks would become Sustain, the fuel on the go, and Dinner would become Refuel, nutrition for another day.

I not only have control of the flow of information, but also now have benefit-led titles for each section and a short explanation that guides me to ensure that the right content goes into this section. At the same time, I've established what this is about as I navigate the audience through my content.

OPTIMISE

Optimising in action

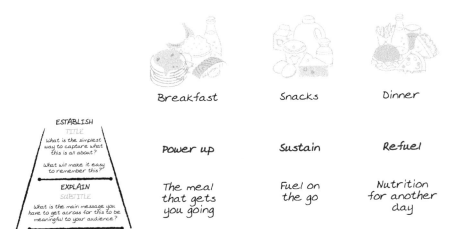

	Breakfast	Snacks	Dinner
	Power up	Sustain	Refuel
	The meal that gets you going	Fuel on the go	Nutrition for another day

ESTABLISH
TITLE
What is the simplest way to capture what this is all about?
What will make it easy to remember this?

EXPLAIN
SUBTITLE
What is the main message you have to get across for this to be meaningful to your audience?

When complete, you will also find the next step of being able to visualise your content on a single page extremely easy, because most of the work will already have been done.

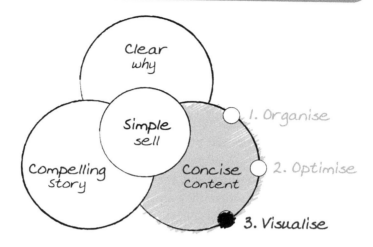

Toolset #3: Visualise

Every presentation can be a presentation on one page.

If you can draw it, you can explain it to anyone. The goal of this set of tools is to be able to create a presentation on a page – the Hero Slide, as I call it.

This final exercise will help you **Visualise** how you deliver the change on a page and be ready to present anywhere at any time with a single slide.

I am sure you have heard the phrase before: a picture paints a thousand words.

This first appeared in a 1911 newspaper article quoting editor Arthur Brisbane's discussion of journalism and publicity: 'Use a picture. It's worth a thousand words.' During the discussion, Brisbane was making a clear-cut case for the use of images to accompany stories.

We process visuals quicker than words, and the brain uses images to aid recall. I am sure you probably use images within your slides, and I cover a lot more about their role within your presentation in the next chapter.

What you want to think about here is the image that can support your entire story, which paints a picture of how you will solve your

VISUALISE

audience's problem at the highest level – being able to visualise the journey through your content to see the change you bring in a way that the audience gets to picture everything on just one page. And this is possible for *every* presentation.

Pictures don't just help form memories; they allow our brains to take in large amounts of information very quickly. They help your audience understand relationships and complex information without the need for detailed explanations; they give context and establish the logical flow that sits above the detail.

They help you as the presenter by giving you the same high-level view of the structure of your content, they help you determine the navigation of your story, and they help the audience see how everything fits together, where they are and what is coming next.

Imagine the value of having all of your content neatly summarised onto one page. What if suddenly there is no room available for the meeting, your laptop dies or is left in the cab? All of this has happened more than once to people I know. You can now draw your core content on a napkin and outline the change you see as possible, and how you move the audience through your main content pillars to land the most important points you need to make, all without a single slide in sight.

If you can draw it, you know you can explain it to anyone, anywhere, anytime.

I'm going to assume you are now convinced by the power of the Hero Slide. And there is more great news; with the work you have already completed in this chapter, it is a simple process to create it.

Step 1: The shape of the relationships

The last step in Organising your content was to establish the order based on the relationships that existed between the groups you have.

Well, that relationship is where you start to build your Hero Slide. That relationship will help you decide what shape and graphical representation will be most appropriate for your content.

On this page is a collection of shapes that relate to the most common types of relationships. Your first job is to decide which of these shapes, based on the relationship you have, is the most effective at demonstrating the journey through your groups – remembering that the goal is always to show how you are taking the audience from Winter to a Better Place in the most logical way.

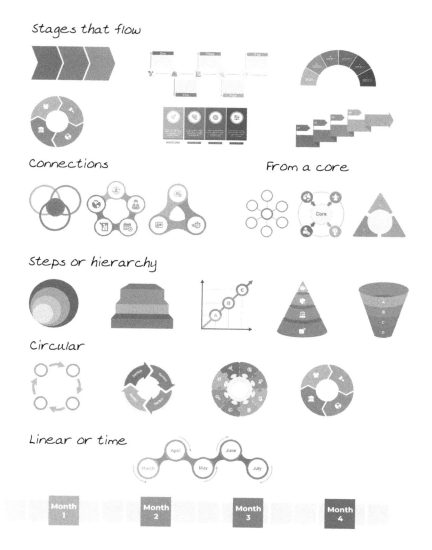

The goal is to find a shape that brings the relationship to life, not to pick a shape you like or you already have on a slide that will be easy to change in PowerPoint. Yes, I know you do that too. Stop it.

And logic remains critical. You want a shape that guides your audience in the best possible way through your content, creating a mental picture of your solution and the relationships that connects your content from this single image.

Step 2: Sketch

Once you have a couple of possible options in mind (maybe you have two relationships that could work or a couple of different shapes that could elevate the understanding of your ideas), grab a couple of sheets of paper and sketch out how they look. Add the words you used to establish what each group is all about, and if you have space on your shape you could also add the main point for each group.

Just get creative for a few minutes and see how things look on paper when you sketch them out. This is a great way to refine the shape to bring to life your content on the page before you commit to drawing this up.

Step 3: Create

Once you are happy you have the right relationship and a shape that brings this to life, you can create a slide that shows how the groups connect and the journey you have to navigate through your content from Winter to your Better Place, demonstrating the change you see as possible.

This is your Hero Slide, your content visualised on one page.

It really is that simple, but I cannot tell you the feedback I get when people master this and get into the habit of doing this for every presentation; it is quite literally a game changer.

It will also save you when you have to present without your presentation, and you can draw your entire solution on a napkin! And, yes, that is also a true story.

If I take my optimised content from earlier, I have two shapes that I think could work based on the relationships between Breakfast, Snacks and Dinner, which I Optimised to become Power Up, Sustain and Refuel.

VISUALISE

I could use a linear timeline approach, or I could have a wheel where they don't just flow logically around but they connect back in a loop, as our eating habits naturally do. And on that basis the loop is, therefore, the most logical and the one I would choose for my Hero Slide. The sketch of this and the final slide are shown below.

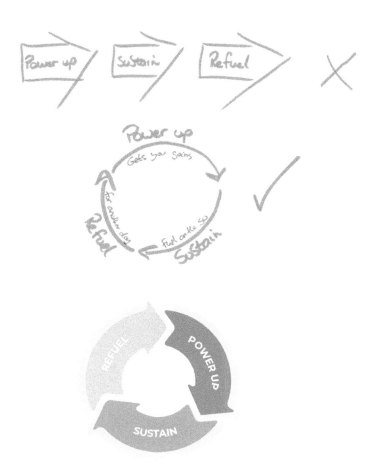

One of the questions I get a lot is should I do this before or after I have built my slide deck?

The answer is both; you want to do this upfront before you get into creating the full slide deck, because this will significantly improve the flow of the slides and how you work on structuring and writing your story in the next chapter. Then you want to go back over this after you have finalised your slide headings and see if there are any changes to make to how you are explaining and establishing what is in each group or section of content as it will become in your final presentation.

As you become practised in this approach, it won't take long to do, and so you will find that doing one at the beginning and checking back and refining at the end will be easy.

Following this before-and-after approach will serve as a tool to support the creation of a compelling story, guide how your content comes into slide order and then be a very valuable tool for you when you set up your presentation. And it gives your audience one slide with everything they need to present your solution as well.

That is why this is the Hero Slide. One day this slide will be your hero and save you.

That is why this is the Hero Slide. One day this slide will be your hero and save you.

Concise content conclusion

Content is the lifeblood of a sales presentation that will keep you in the game.

In this chapter you have learned that complexity is not your friend, and that you need to prepare your presentations to make it easy for people to buy your finished product. I call this selling the dish not the ingredients. So, it's time to make sure your presentations don't take the market stall approach and give the audience all of your offerings for them to pick at like a seagull and choose the odd chip they fancy.

You must also remember you decide what people see and when. Ladder your content to help your audience follow along, make your key points clear and bold, and ensure you define what you want them to take away and how to find what they need to take your ideas forward. Always ask what information must you get across to the audience, and what is support or secondary or could be dropped if you have too much content.

Some people find this hard to believe, but *every* presentation can be a whittled down to one page. Yes, every presentation. If you cannot do this, you are not clear enough on who your target audience is and how your content delivers a change that **they** need. Getting to this level of clarity means you will be ready to present anywhere, to anyone in any circumstances.

When you apply these tools to your content you will become a lot more confident in how you bring your audience into your story right from the outset.

In the next toolbox you will learn how to bring together everything you have done so far to craft a compelling story, which will help your audience take in and remember what you share with them.

TOOLBOX 3:
COMPELLING STORY

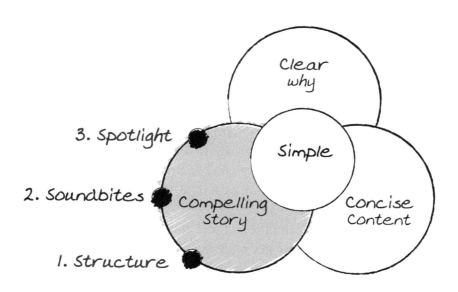

3. Spotlight

2. Soundbites

1. Structure

Compelling
Story

Clear
why

Simple

Concise
Content

SOFTWARE SUCKS FOR STORYTELLING

Until this point, your work will have been primarily focused on getting ready for the main act, the part where your content meets your audience and they see it in front of them for the first time. You get one shot to get your message across and land that vital connection when delivering the content. You are there to get an outcome; what could go wrong?

Your presentation will almost certainly be delivered using some form of presentation software, be that PowerPoint, Keynote, Prezi, Google slides or similar.

Let's face it, they all have myriad issues that make them suck in helping you out right now, and you have probably learned and adapted to work around some of these limitations and time-sucking frustrations. You 'might' grab slides from existing decks, even if they don't quite fit. Dog food, cat food – huh, both pets, it kind of works, leave the image, change the heading to make a new point, insert, done.

The lure of the slide deck is too great to resist and you fall into the trap of starting to create slides as the way to pull things together. Once you start, you keep adding slide after slide and never step back to see the mess you have created. This only becomes apparent as you try to present it, now finding it hard to recall all the points you need to make and what each slide is there to do, let alone what might pop up next: *Oh, that slide, I thought I had deleted that one or shoved it into the appendix in the cab ride over here ...* A nice surprise for you and the audience.

The audience looks a little lost and confused too. What is on the slides and your words are not quite in sync. You narrated a beautiful audience insight demonstrating your expertise with hipsters and establishing a sense of belonging; the client is enthralled. This key slide is titled 'Why us?', with a picture of a bearded hipster dude with a very cool motorbike, a long list of bullet points heavy with percentages, and a little bar chart showing how many hipsters you can reach. It was a stroke of genius getting so much information on one slide, even if it is now almost impossible to read any of it.

A week later, when the client searches for this great insight, they get lost in the presentation and they can't quite remember what you said or what the point of the 'Why us?' slide was. What a waste of all that great work.

Or slides have come from all over the organisation, there doesn't seem to be an agreed style or way of putting slides together, and it is clear, even to the untrained eye, that this is not one presentation but many with a failed attempt to mask the joins with some section dividers to try to divert attention away from the layout changes and some questionable font choices by one of the many teams that have contributed to this patchwork quilt of content.

The sections don't flow seamlessly from one to the next; they jump and jerk like a heavy train lugging coal up a steep section of track, with the same degree of elegance. It is hard to stay interested and connected, let alone follow along.

And then you hit the section full of your favourite tools; your internal jargon and three-letter acronyms are emblazoned proudly across the slides as if everyone knows this internal code. As you present, you know these things so well that you fly past them, rattling off one TLA and then another.

Sadly, your audience doesn't know this code anywhere near as well as you and are heading straight for the rocks. They would prefer their rocks to come with a gin and tonic about now. They become ever more confused, overwhelmed and easily distracted by ... oh look, a pigeon.

You love your ideas, how you came up with them, and how they work; in fact, so much to the point that there is a slide heading 'Why we love it' – glad you do! The audience meanwhile searches for meaning; they may be so distracted that they are thinking about the meaning of life right now, or what does this mean to us, an hour we will never get back? This all looks fab and fancy, but what do we do with this, and what does it do for us?

And then to end it all – oh please, can it end? – a couple of pages of actions and next steps suggest that working together will take more effort than the audience can spare since they are exhausted.

Some terms and conditions then follow, spelling out a few limitations the audience should be aware of that might make some of the things they have just seen hard or impossible to deliver.

COMPELLING

Thank you, says the last slide. And it's over. For which everyone is grateful.

Maybe this sounds like I have been watching you create and deliver your last few presentations; I haven't, but I have had to deal with the consequences and impact of these things for years and, sadly, I still see way too many of these issues every week, particularly when I hear:

▶ I hope they can follow along and we don't lose them.

▶ I hope I can land all the key points and not get lost in the slides.

▶ I hope we don't spend too much time just talking about us.

▶ I hope they can remember what this is all about when they come back to review our content in a few days.

What if there was a way to:

▶ simplify what you say to aid your recall of the critical points you need to make for you and the audience

▶ help your audience follow what you are saying even though they have never seen this content before and have no idea what is coming next

▶ help them recall and find critical pieces of information, not just the next day but over weeks, possibly even months

▶ help them remember what you said so they could confidently present this to others after you have left

▶ connect them to you and your content

▶ connect across an audience with a range of different learning styles

▶ connect with depth and emotion

▶ move your audience to action?

Does that sound impossible to you?

Well, it's not if you combine everything you have learnt so far with the tools to become an effective storyteller.

WHY STORIES MATTER

What is this picture all about?

Ever heard the phrase: a bird in the hand is worth two in the bush?

This is a proverb, and it warns us against giving up something we already have, speculating that there could be something better around the corner. This is a very simple tale, but it packs quite a punch in terms of the meaning behind the words.

And what's more, it has some history; this was taken from the Aesop fable 'The Hawk and The Nightingale', written in 570 BCE. The hawk said: 'I would be foolish to release a bird I have in my hand to pursue another bird that is not even in sight.'

So how come a story from over 2500 years ago still exists in every language and culture today?

Daniel Siegel, who is a clinical professor of psychiatry at UCLA, can help shed some light on this from his work studying this area: 'Research shows that we remember details much more effectively when embedded in a story. Telling and being moved to action by them is in our DNA.' Put simply, we are wired for stories. It is how we receive, process and store what we hear, and how we draw meaning and relevance.

COMPELLING

And this proverb is an excellent example of how stories can stand the test of time and help us convey detailed information in a simplified narrative. Right back to before we could speak in modern language, we used carvings to tell stories – stories of where food was, where danger was, where tribes were located. Stories are how we learn and take on new information, and how we share what we have learnt with others. Our brain loves a good story.

In his book *The Science of Storytelling*, Will Storr suggests recent research points to stories being how language evolved, principally to swap 'social information' back when we lived in Stone Age tribes. In other words, we'd gossip. We'd tell tales about the moral rights and wrongs of other people, punish bad behaviour, reward good and thereby keep everyone cooperating and the tribe in check.

His research suggests we're wired to tell stories, enjoy them and connect through them. And Will isn't the only person to think or have researched this. Psychologist Professor Jonathan Haidt describes the human mind as a 'story processor, not a logic processor. Everyone loves a good story; every culture bathes its children in stories'.

Organisational psychologist Peg Neuhauser found that learning which stems from a well-told story is remembered more accurately and for far longer than learning derived purely from facts and figures. Similarly, psychologist Jerome Bruner's research suggests that facts are 20 times more likely to be remembered if they're part of a story.

Finally, in making my point here, let me share a story from *Made to Stick*, a book about why some ideas stick and some don't. In their research, Chip and Dan Heath conducted an experiment with Stanford University students. The students were given one minute to make a speech about crime stats in the US, either saying things were getting worse or there was nothing to worry about.

As you'd expect, these are smart students. They also tend to be quick thinkers and good communicators. No-one in the room ever gives a poor speech. After each speech, the listeners rated the speaker: how impressive was the delivery? How persuasive? As you would imagine, the most polished speakers get the highest ratings. No surprise, right – you would expect good speakers to score well in speaking contests.

The exercise appears to be over – but they are then asked to pull out a sheet of paper and write down every idea they remember for each speaker they heard. The students are quite taken aback by how little they remember – only ten minutes have elapsed since the speeches were given. And they've heard only eight one-minute speeches.

Most students are lucky to recall one or two ideas from each presentation. Many draw a complete blank – unable to remember a single concept from some of the speeches. In the average one-minute speech, the typical student uses 2.5 statistics. Only one student in ten tells a story.

Although most students use stats rather than stories, 63% remember the stories, while only 5% remember an individual data point. This experiment reinforces that stories are much easier to recall than factual, detailed stats.

Now, just take a moment to think about your last set of slides; what was more prominent, a well-crafted story or a collection of slides containing a lot of facts, stats and data points?

Are you convinced yet?

TURNING YOU INTO A STORYTELLER

Coming up in this toolbox, you will learn how to create a presentation that is designed to deliver your content through a compelling story with three new tools that will guide you to:

▸ **Structure** your presentation around a three-stage story arc specifically designed for selling ideas

▸ ensure that the **Soundbites** of the story are the most prominent and visible within your content and slides

▸ shine the **Spotlight** on why this matters and what is in it for the audience.

COMPELLING

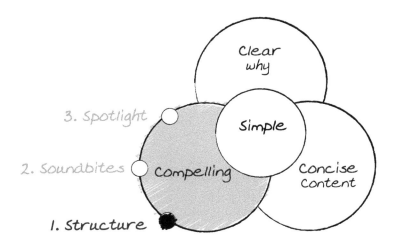

It's only a story because it was designed to be one.

Having established that stories are a powerful way to bring your content to life, how does a story get structured, what elements are needed to deliver these benefits, and how does this translate to how you build your presentations?

You see, it's not enough to know the impact of stories. You need to know what makes a story work and, more importantly, what makes your presentation work as a story.

If you Google 'story structure', be prepared to lose a week or two down a deep rabbit hole of opinions and points of view, most of which are irrelevant to what you need to achieve here. You will most likely emerge none the wiser, just a little overwhelmed perhaps. I did a six-week story writing course; trust me, you don't need to do that either, because most of this was also irrelevant for what we need here.

> You need to know what makes a story work and, more importantly, what makes your presentation work as a story.

LET'S BEGIN WITH A LITTLE STORY

There was a young lady with evil sisters and an awful life.

Sadly, misery awaits her.

She gets an invitation to the ball from a prince. She makes clothes for the ball.

She goes to the ball and dances with the prince.

But, oh no, she has to go.

And it's back to an awful life with the evil sisters.

But, wait, the prince finds her, and they live happily ever after.

Do you know the story?

Yes, of course, it is Cinderella.

STORY STRUCTURE: Cinderella

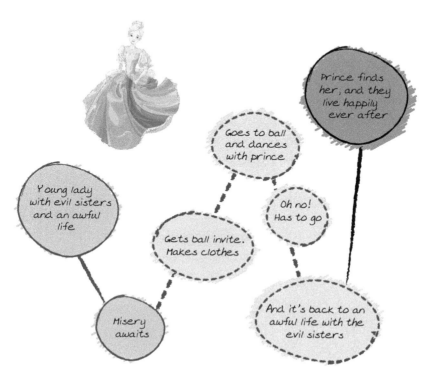

Now, let me ask you this:

- ► What stands out about this? Anything you notice?
- ► Do you think this is unique to Cinderella?
- ► Why do you think this works?

This particular story starts off by establishing the premise of the story, the young girl with the problem of the evil sisters.

It quickly slips down into a darker place, the misery that awaits Cinderella, and draws us in, giving us a reason to care and feel part of something; together, we hope for a better future. We hope she can escape to a better life.

We then move through the story with some highs and lows, navigating our way through until finally, there is a resolution, a conclusive ending – in this case, a happy one, rewarding us and giving us a reason to have gone on this journey.

Is this unique to the story of Cinderella?

No, behind this tale is a story structure I have simplified a little further for this book but which is common to the vast majority of fiction books and movies.

The way this story arc works is by **establishing** the context of the story before moving to the main part of the story, which is **navigated** through some ups and downs before there is a **resolution** which, in this instance, concludes on a high point.

When you step back, you can see the story of Cinderella follows these three core stages.

What changes from story to story, the creative licence if you like, is this centre section of how they navigate and take you through the ups and downs and, of course, where the writer decides to take you and whether the story ends well or not. You will now start to notice this as you watch your next blockbuster movie or start a novel.

STORY STRUCTURE: Stages

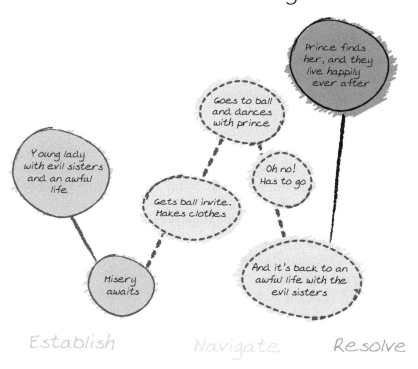

Establish   Navigate   Resolve

YOUR PRESENTATION AS A STORY

Now for the purposes of making your presentation work as a story, there are a couple of elements of this arc that you either don't need or don't want in your story structure, and some critical parts of this story arc that will guide you to become a masterful story creator.

Let's unpack what it is that will turn your presentation into a compelling, flowing story.

We start by **establishing** the story: there is a goal, blocked by a problem. What's at stake, and how bad could this get? Give the audience a reason to care, join in and feel part of this.

Unspoken connection: together, we hope for a better future (which is the change you see as being possible: your Winter to Better Place).

Then we **navigate** your audience to a resolution with a narrative and navigation that **they can easily follow along with**.

Now, this is where things differ a little between movies and the presentation types that this book deals with. In movies, the writer will play with emotional highs and lows, as happens in Cinderella. There may be several rolling arcs within the one story, huge highs and massive lows, characters being killed off and new heroes coming in to save the day.

However, when your goal is to share content that you need your audience to understand, follow and be able to share with others, this roller-coaster of drama is the last thing you want or need.

You want to get from your low point to your resolution with speed, ease and complete clarity.

Logic is your best friend, not theatrics and drama.

In Cinderella, Winter (A) is an awful life and the Better Place (B) is living happily ever after.

For this book it is Hopeful Presenter (A) to Strategic Storyteller (B), which we are navigating through now.

In the Concise ingredients example, it is Nutritionally Vacant (A) to Energised Seller (B).

In each case, the navigation of the story needs to get the audience from point A to B as cleanly and logically as possible.

Then there is the **resolution**.

This is very important because this tells the audience how things conclude. Did they get what they had hoped for and what they became invested in at the outset? Did the character you fell in love with live or die? Have we reached a Better Place than where we started? That is what we all wanted, right?

Ever had a movie that didn't resolve, the ending wasn't clear or there was no conclusive ending at all? What happened to them? Did they survive and overcome evil? Did they find true love? Did she escape her evil sisters for a better life?

Imagine if the prince never came back. How does that story feel if it ended after Cinderella leaves the ball? How about if, just after she left the ball, there were some next steps for how the prince can find Cinderella for them to live happily ever after, a few limitations and outstanding actions points and then a couple of pages of terms and conditions? *What?* That sounds ridiculous; nobody would ever end a story like that.

Have a look at your last couple of presentations. This is what I see far too often. An inconclusive ending, never quite landing the plane or

STRUCTURE

getting the audience to that promised outcome. Instead, there might be an odd summary that was thrown together in the cab because it didn't feel like there was an endpoint, a list of next steps or the good old 'thank you' slide. Nothing says I didn't know how to end this story better than a thank you slide.

And here is the other difference to our movie story arc: all of your presentations should land on a conclusive high. There should be a clear resolution, and it should be positive. You can't leave your audience in Winter.

We need to end at a place that is better than where we started. In my experience, tragic endings aren't great when trying to convince someone to buy into your solution. No, that final slide should clearly express that this (Better Place) is where you can take them.

And you can probably already see that these sections are not balanced; the largest section is the navigation, and this is where the bulk of your content will reside. More on that in moment.

ADDING CONTENT TO THE STORY – WHAT GOES WHERE?

Having established that this is the three-stage story structure that *every* presentation should follow, how does the work you have done so far work with this, and where does all of your content go?

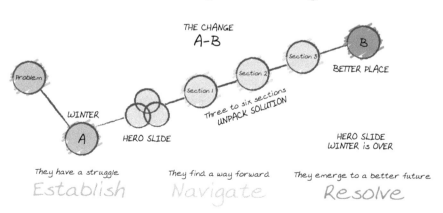

The three-stage sales story arc

First up, the change you defined in the chapter on Getting Clear when you worked through your Winter (A) to a Better Place (B) guides your overall story. The Problem into Winter is the low point of establishing the story, point A, to the high point of the story at the resolution, point B. Your Hero Slide establishes the navigation before you unpack the content in the sections that follow the logic of this visual. And then your Hero Slide can also help you summarise the change your content delivers in your conclusive and positive resolution.

Establishing the story

You begin establishing your story with their problem; this is their goal, and they want this solved.

Next comes the Winter you have defined for this presentation; what's at stake, and how bad could this get without your solution? You are establishing there is a struggle, and you are bringing the audience into this story, which now really matters to them.

There is now an unspoken connection: together, you both hope for a better future.

Navigating the story

This is where the bulk of your slides will live and where your solution will be delivered; however, there are some critical structural elements to this that need to be followed to establish interest and then keep your audience on the same path as you. The path from Winter to the Better Place.

As a pilot I am acutely aware of the need to plan a flight and be very precise with navigation. Getting lost is a recipe for disaster. The same is true of presentations, and to me it can be very obvious when either the presenter or the audience is lost. More often than not, within a few of minutes of this realisation, a few more slides in, the impending disaster becomes clear to all.

Navigation is quite simply about knowing where you want to go from and to, where you are and where next. When everyone is clear on that and can follow along, there will be no more getting lost in a sea of slides that aren't helping anyone.

Clear navigation starts by setting up how you are going to step through what is coming.

STRUCTURE

Setting up the navigation

First up, you want to provide an overview of what is coming up, the flow through the core part of your content. This is where your Hero Slide comes in. This slide can be used to overview how you are going to move from the Winter you have just delivered and arrive at the Better Place you want to take your audience to. It is the map of the route through your presentation.

Clear navigation starts by setting up how you are going to step through what is coming. This will help you stay on course, not present out of sequence or get ahead of your content, a surefire way to lose your audience.

Now, your Hero Slide that overviews the navigation for this journey is *not* an agenda. It is not simply a list of sections. It is how your story unfolds, guided by the relationships that form logical connections. An agenda is just a list of content in the order in which you have put it together. These are *not* the same thing.

The core content of this book is built around four sections that are on my Hero Slide, which shows the relationship of these sections. In the final chapter on Simple, you will see how those tools are formed from the intersections of the other three chapters. This is not an agenda; it is a carefully designed tool to help you and your audience navigate through the content together, staying aligned, connected and on the same path.

The Hero Slide for this book. How you are navigating through the content.

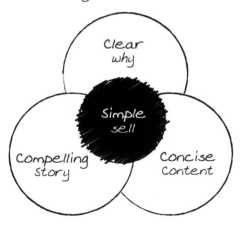

There is one word of caution with the Hero Slide and the setup of your navigation. Its purpose is to establish how you are going to move through the content, three to six sections that will be named and signposted in the same way as the names on your Hero Slide. You must avoid revealing the whole presentation at this point, verging from establishing the essence of this section with the short explanation to finding yourself explaining all the detail within each section. Stop at the high-level overview of each section; otherwise, you will present the whole presentation on a slide and then present it again to an increasingly frustrated and possibly confused audience.

The only time you present 'everything' on the Hero Slide is when that is your only slide. When it is used to set up the navigation, establish what each section is about and then get into presenting the core content of the first section.

Creating the sections and signalling where you are

Having set up the navigation with the Hero Slide, you now need to ensure your content follows this order and you make it as clear as possible where you are in the presentation.

Personally, I am a big advocate of section slides or even using the Hero Slide to signal where in the story you are and what is coming next. Again, this book follows that format, and in a big presentation, this is critical to avoid losing your audience as your transition between sections. You can use this to summarise what you have just covered before setting up where you are going next.

However you choose to do this or your organisation's presentation templates dictate, having set up the navigation, you must now ensure your audience is never left wondering where they are, and that when they pick up your presentation in two weeks it's just as easy to find their way around your content.

Again, just to be clear, if your Hero Slide has three sections – for example, Power Up, Sustain and Refuel – these are the three sections of your presentation that follow your Hero Slide after setting this up as the navigation. Signpost the start of each new section either with the Hero Slide or a section divider. In a big presentation, use the change of section as a way to summarise what you have just presented and set up what is coming next. This will help both you and the audience stay connected and follow along. This gives you a moment to catch your breath and prepare for the next section coming up; you can also use this moment to check in with your audience, asking them what is resonating to check understanding but also to see how your story is landing with them, what is standing out and what they recall. Checking in means you can ensure they are ready to move on and are not still hung up on something that will prevent them from staying present with you as you move forward into this new section.

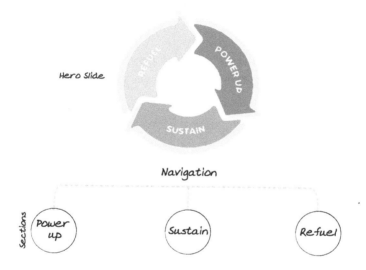

Each of these sections, signalled by the Hero Slide, will contain a selection of slides that unpack the content relevant to that section. In the Soundbites tool coming up, I will cover how to ensure the key points you need to make within each section stand out and are easy to spot within your slides.

Resolution

Now you have navigated through all of your content, you need to conclude this journey by cementing that you have been able to show the way to a Better Place. There should be no doubt after you present these final couple of slides that you have demonstrated you can solve their bigger problem, that of Winter.

This is one, maybe two slides by way of a conclusive summary of what you see as being possible through your solution. You can use the Hero Slide again here; however, this time, rather than narrating the journey ahead, you are going to use this to reinforce that what you have just shared in each of these sections together solves their problem and moves them from Winter to the Better Place. This can be as simple as adding a summary stating just that. For example:

> We have demonstrated that by learning how to create presentations that are Clear, Concise, Compelling and Simple, you can go from being a Hopeful Presenter to a Strategic Storyteller.

Or:

> Our journey through how to Power Up, Sustain and Refuel has shown how the most Nutritionally Vacant salesperson can become an Energised Seller.

The key is you confidently state the change and highlight what you have shared is how that change becomes possible. That is what your resolution is there to do, make it clear you have emerged to a better future. Your resolution should always come before any next steps or special considerations, terms, conditions and so on. Complete the story before getting into those nuts-and-bolts details.

One final point to note on the Resolution is that you should not introduce new content or ideas at this point. It should be a one- or two-page conclusive summary of the journey you have taken the audience on from Winter through your content. It is not the time to try to land one more idea. If it wasn't covered in your content, it shouldn't be part of your Resolution.

I do get asked why you can't just take the order you created when you organised your groups in the Concise Content chapter and use this to lay out your story. Why does it need a whole new structure?

You absolutely can use that, and it will certainly make a difference; as you have seen, this does form part of the story navigation but it is just one element. The power of the story structure is to expand the logic you have at the core of your content flow and extend this out to draw the audience in, to give them a reason to care about your content and to feel part of your story right upfront.

You do that before navigating through the content, by establishing why this matters to them in the form of your cold and dark wintery place, and then after you have been through how you deliver the change, you tie this off with a bow that clarifies why this matters and what is in it for them. These two quick extra steps take you from just having structured navigation to creating a flowing story that brings the audience in and keeps them engaged as you work through unpacking the content to eventually reach the resolution they were hoping for.

Those who have been trained in this approach tell me that having a structure specifically designed for selling solutions has changed how they frame their content in this way, ensuring these two key bookends of the story are present, taking them from having a nice content layout to establishing a structure that leads to a compelling story which forms deeper and more lasting connections.

STRUCTURE

Story structure

Establish	Navigate	Resolve
They have a struggle	They find a way forward	They emerge to a better future
There is a goal, blocked by a problem. What's at stake, how bad could this get? *Unspoken: together we hope for a better future*	How will our audience move through the story to a resolution?	Did we get what we had hoped for at the outset? Did it happen or not? Have we reached a better place than where we started from?
Getting the audience to feel that they are in your story, they are the character	*Guiding them on a clear path through your solution*	*Highlighting that you have solved the bigger problem*
WINTER IS COMING	**HERO SLIDE THEN SOLUTION**	**HERO SLIDE ARRIVED AT THE BETTER PLACE**

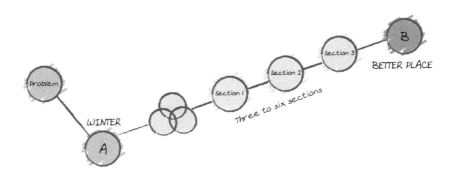

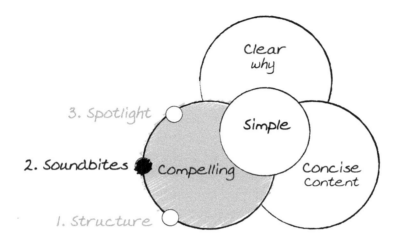

The story in the headlines.

Now you have the three-stage story arc of Establish, Navigate and Resolve worked out, it is time to build on this and enhance how you deliver content by getting down into the format of slides that are inevitably going to be part of your delivery method. You can't forget the slides.

Soundbites are all about how you take the content sections that live within your navigation and move from the high-level sections down into the narrative that will connect your key points, and then how this flows through to form a story within the slide itself.

> **You need to control what the audience sees and in what order they see it.**

Yes, your slides need a story too. It is not just a case of taking content, throwing it onto slides and hoping it connects, having set up what is coming up where within the story structure. You need to control what the audience sees and in what order they see it. You want to place emphasis on the important points; you want to direct them to what you want them to give their attention to and emphasise what you want them to take away.

'That slide showing 62%, was that good or bad for us? I can't remember, it looks bad now, but I think they said it was good.' This is what you have to avoid.

You want them to be able to easily recall the point you make on each slide as well as how you can help them find what they need in all of your content after you leave. This is a key element of what your story structure delivers, but your slides need to play their part in this too.

If you have worked through the exercises in the Concise Content chapter to organise and optimise your content, you will be well prepared for this and find this very quick and easy to apply. If not, this will still help you bring organisation to your content within the critical delivery of navigating the audience from your view of Winter (A) to your Better Place (B), or the resolution as it appears in the story structure.

COFFEE LABELS TO POWERPOINT SLIDES VIA BRAIN SCIENCE

Believe it or not, I know a thing or two about label design. I know secrets like this are hard to keep to yourself.

This all started when I was designing labels for a flavoured coffee company in the UK. Actually, this isn't quite true. I started to learn when the UK's largest supermarket chain, Sainsbury's, refused to stock our products until we changed the labels. The labels I had designed.

Now for some context. I was a 15 year old with some design software looking for cash to fund an expensive habit. Learning to fly. The company made great coffee but had no idea about design, which is what we had in common, but I could use this fancy design software and got myself a side hustle.

When this feedback came in, the team were nervous to say my designs sucked, but since I hadn't really designed them (I just moved some things around in the software until they looked 'cool'), when

I found out I wasn't devastated. Instead, I saw an opportunity. An opportunity to learn what a label should actually look like.

I suggested we sit down with the supermarket giant's team and learn 'what their requirements were', meaning learn what actually makes a good label, because I knew nothing about this but was keen to find out. I'll come back to this story and what I learnt in those early days in a moment.

Fast-forward 20 odd years, and I am now the managing director of a shopper marketing agency with three offices across Australia and New Zealand, working with the likes of P&G, Pernod Ricard and the supermarket chain Woolworths on strategies to engage shoppers and influence shopping behaviour. (I did not pursue a design career, you might be surprised to hear.)

We were working with some of the leading minds in the application of neuroscience and eye-tracking technology, using brain imaging to understand how we actually process, store and recall information. We also took advantage of advances in behavioural science and the application of psychology to marketing. Now this isn't a marketing science book but here are some relevant learnings for what is coming next.

We naturally scan for information; as we do this, our eyes follow a pattern that scans and pauses when we read. We learnt that eyes typically scan across a label between seven and nine words before we need to pause to process what was being read.

It's scientifically better to break up the text into a series of shorter lines to create the natural pauses needed for visual processing. When customers are scanning shelves for a product, they'll be significantly more likely to choose a label they can grasp in the first scan. You don't have long to gain and hold attention.

Peter Steidl, author of *Neurobranding* and whom I worked with during this time, would say, 'Images and emotions are the languages of the mind; in marketing, we rely far too much on words'. This is because we process visuals quicker than words. The brain uses images to aid recall, so adding imagery to a product label is a short cut to getting noticed and creating a code within the memory that the brain can quickly access to make meaning of what we see.

SOUNDBITES

The brain is also strongly influenced by the order in which we read information. It wants to make up a story (remember that our brain is wired for stories) about what it sees and how it 'goes together', and it also wants this story to be consistent with what it saw first. The headline and the subpoint and any images all need to be congruent; they need to make one clear point. Ah, there is logic again – your friend.

When we can't quickly make sense of something, when it doesn't flow logically, when multiple elements don't quite connect, our brain goes from subconscious processing of information into conscious processing, which requires effort and energy. Doing Sudoku for an hour is much more taxing than reading a cartoon. You don't want to exhaust your audience by making them think; in fact, quite the opposite. You want to make any choices as automatic as possible.

One important point here is that because we are wired for stories and this is how the brain stores and recalls information, when there are gaps in a story, our brain will simply fill them in. In other words, it will make up its own story to get everything to make sense, even if that takes a bit of brain power. Now think about that for a second; if you don't make the story in your presentation and across your slides crystal clear and easy to understand, your audience will make up their own version. That could be really bad for you.

So the hierarchy of information, especially for the first three items in a sequence, is critical, as is the fact that they are all connected.

Now back to what I learnt during my coffee label adventures …

After the meeting with the supermarket buyers and their marketing team, my labels were designed around these simple principles:

- ► The biggest thing should be the most important.
- ► The next two things need to support that.
- ► Everything else is irrelevant and shouldn't get in the way of the first two.

Basic as this was, it served me well, and it was a very proud moment when I saw my coffee labels on the shelves, and an even better moment when we got our second order to keep us there. People found and purchased my labels. They probably wanted the beautiful flavoured coffee, but it was the label that made all the difference; at least, that's what I told myself.

What does this have to do with your slides? Well, I have learned that these principles also apply to slide layout; the hierarchy and the layout of the information on the slide matter a lot.

Nancy Duarte authored a book called *Slide:ology*, which is all about slide layout and design. She writes:

> Quite possibly, how slides are arranged has the most impact on whether a slide's message is visually clear.
>
> Arrangement tells a story. Based on the arrangement decisions a designer makes, a slide can prompt feelings of tension, confusion, and agitation; conversely, it can maximise clarity by employing the following:
>
> - Contrast: The audience can identify the main point quickly.
> - Flow: The audience knows the order in which to process the information.
> - Hierarchy: The audience sees the relationship between elements.
> - Unity: The audience senses that the information belongs together.
> - Proximity: The audience perceives meaning from the location of elements.
> - White space: The audience has visual breathing room.
>
> These are the tools of the slide design trade. It's tough to assemble a great slide without paying close attention to each of these issues.

One of the things I love about my work as a strategist is that when multiple credible sources of information from different areas converge, align and illuminate a path, they paint a clear picture of the best way forward, and that was certainly the case when I began pulling this all together many years ago.

SOUNDBITES

SLIDE SOUNDBITES: WHAT MATTERS

So here's what I have taken from being a 15-year-old coffee label designer combined with several hundred million dollars of market-leading marketing research and a book dedicated to slide layout (I can feel the suspense):

> ▸ **First scan:** The biggest and most prominent should be the most important.
>
> ▸ **Connected short cuts:** The role of the picture, chart or graphic on a slide is to support the main point. It is a short cut to make the point stick.
>
> ▸ **Order of three:** Order matters up to three, and then just don't distract from those three.

First scan

The first scan is critical. This will take in what looks most important, such as the biggest font, or is most prominent, such as the top line. So this is where the main point should be, which on most slides should be the headline. But on most slides, this is wasted on something completely irrelevant or unrelated to the main point, such as 'Our approach', 'The insights' or 'Why we love this'.

Make the most important point look the most important using size and placement.

> **Make the most important point look the most important using size and placement.**

Connected short cuts

Images are short cuts when they connect. Images should support the most important point, and not just be a placeholder or a nice image you found that relates to the whole topic of the presentation.

There is a school of thought that images on slides should be abstract, creative and arty. I am not from that school. Everything I have studied, researched, experienced in the real world and seen work contradicts this for the style of presentations I work with. That is to say that in some instances this approach might be useful, but when it comes to taking an audience on a journey through content that needs a life beyond this one presentation, this isn't the case.

The role of the picture, chart or graphic on a slide is to support the main point. It is a short cut to make the point stick. That is its most important role. After that, creativity, beauty and any artistic filters can be applied, but if the image does not connect with the slide's main point, delete it. Simple.

Order of three

The most important point is followed by the second and third most important points, and then, well, what comes next doesn't get much attention at all but you do want to avoid it distracting from the important stuff, so don't have point four in a font six times larger than the most important point!

It is important you take control of how you bring the story to life and the point *you* want to make on each and every slide. Take control of the story the audience hears and what you want them to recall.

Let's step through how to ensure the Soundbites of your story help you sell your solution.

The first thing that helps you get the best possible structure into your slides is to know your overarching narrative first, and the absolute best way to do this is away from slides. Yes, I know there is a beautiful contradiction in there. To make your slides really work for you and help you land your compelling story, stay away from the slides.

Let me explain

Slides can be a distraction. They draw you into working on things such as images, layout and font sizes, which only matter once the point of the slide is well and truly understood, and you know the role of that slide, of that piece of content and the slides are in roughly the right order. Then, and only then, should you go to work on the slide itself.

SOUNDBITES

Without your narrative in hand, getting distracted by slide design and losing your flow will almost certainly happen.

The other gotcha with working on slides before you are clear on your narrative is you become reluctant to let certain slides go later on. I get this all the time when I am coaching and working with people on specific presentations. It can become quite 'animated'. I want to delete a slide because it serves no purpose or is even distracting, and it keeps coming back from the trash and going back into the deck because the creator 'loves that slide'.

What has happened is they have found a great image, they have worked hard on getting the image and the text to work, and the slide does look great. It is just a pointless slide that adds no value to the overall story, but they can't see that because they have become so invested in how nice it looks. This is what happens when you work on the slides before you know your story.

If you want to check your slide Soundbites at any stage, here is a very simple but incredibly powerful exercise. Grab a blank sheet of paper and write down the most prominent point on each slide you have as a list of bullet points. If the slide heading is the leading point, write that down. If there are no slide headings, what is the main point that stands out to you on this slide? Capture this. You want to go for a list of at least 15 points from 15 slides. If you have someone you can share this with, ask them if you can read them the list. When you have finished, ask them what they think your presentation is about, what they recall and what they will take away from this. This will quickly indicate where you need to make changes to ensure your slides are telling the story you want them to tell.

There is discipline needed here.

NARRATIVE AND HIGHLIGHTS

Narrative and highlights are the key to developing effective slide Soundbites.

If you have worked through Toolbox 2 to create Concise content, it is an easy step to now create your overall narrative.

Step 1: Creating the narrative

	POWER UP	SUSTAIN	REFUEL
HERO SLIDE			
ESTABLISH			
EXPLAIN	The meal that gets you going	Fuel on the go	Nutrition for another day
NARRATIVE	Write the longer story that you want to share within each section away from slides. What would you share if we were chatting? What is the storyboard for this presentation?		
HIGHLIGHTS			
SOUNDBITES			

SOUNDBITES

The **narrative** is where you expand on what you are going to say within each section. Think of it like the storyboard of your presentation. When you were introduced to the story of Cinderella on page 163 you could see the storyboard, the high-level story laid out on a page. If you were shooting a movie, would you start by getting your story worked out or go straight to shooting scenes, spending millions on actors and crew only to find out later that what you have doesn't quite make sense? Think of creating slides as shooting the movie. They cost you time to find images, write content and create good-looking layouts; save this for when you have your story refined and ready for shooting.

What is interesting about the Cinderella storyboard is that there are just 48 words on there. And yet you get a very good idea of the story, what each part of the movie is about, what you can expect to see at each part of the journey through that story – and this could be for a movie that is 1 hour and 52 minutes and a book that is over 400 pages. So, if it is possible to produce a 400-page book from a narrative that is under 50 words you should be able to capture the story of your 60-page presentation in under 50 words too.

THE STORYBOARD OF YOUR PRESENTATION

You have established the title of each of the sections of your presentation and given these an explainer in the form of a subtitle. Now imagine we were having a chat, and I asked you what section two of your presentation is about, the section titled Refuel. What would you say? That is your narrative: the summary you have in your head of what you want to get across is what you now want to get out and onto paper.

The narrative is formed by writing down what you want to say for each section of your presentation. Just write down, in plain and simple language, what you want to get across when you present this. It might be one or two paragraphs, or six bullets. It doesn't matter. What matters is that your narrative becomes clear before your slides get out of control. However, your narrative is not your script, it is not the full unabridged story in all its glory, and it is not your slide notes that remind you of everything you want to say on each slide. No, you are adding just enough detail to the work you have already done to make it clear what each section of your presentation delivers and how this flows from section to section. It is the storyboard of your presentation.

At this stage, what you have in the form of slides, existing content, beautiful images, charts, stats – all of this matters a lot less than knowing what it is you want to get across in a flowing, logical story within each section. It is that simple, and once you have this you can move slides around to match this story. I promise you that based on all the feedback I have had from clients over the years, this makes organising slides so much quicker and easier. Slides have a magic power to draw you in and take several hours away from you just making them look better – just before you decide you no longer need that slide.

Create your narrative first and you will save hours later but, more importantly, you will have a clear, logical and flowing story that will help you present and land your key points on each slide.

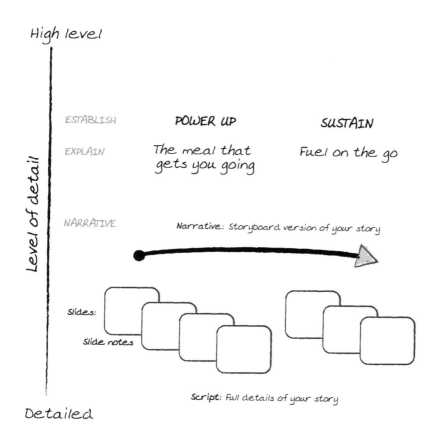

Step 2: Capturing the highlights

	POWER UP	SUSTAIN	REFUEL
HERO SLIDE			
ESTABLISH			
EXPLAIN	The meal that gets you going	Fuel on the go	Nutrition for another day
NARRATIVE	Write the longer story that you want to share within each section away from slides. What would you share if we were chatting? What is the storyboard for this presentation?		
HIGHLIGHTS	Highlight the most important points that need to be landed within each section		
SOUNDBITES			

When you have an overview in narrative form for each section of your presentation, you can then determine what you must get across – the key points you need your audience to hear, see, be able to recall and find again in your slides. These are your highlights.

If you have captured your narrative in a document, you can go through this with a highlighter and pick out the key points. Like marking up a textbook, you don't want to end up with almost everything highlighted; that is pointless. Yes, you want to get that story across, and you want to land your narrative, but what you are looking to ascertain is this: within each section, what must your audience understand? What are the most important points that, if missed or misunderstood, could derail your entire presentation? Highlight or write these down for each section of your presentation.

> When you have an overview in narrative form for each section of your presentation, you can then determine what you must get across ... These are your highlights.

NUMBERS NEED CONTEXT

This is also where you want to think about any charts, data points, research or statistics you might be thinking of using to make, emphasise or support key points. Before you get caught up in slide design, ensure you are clear on what you need the audience to know and what you want them to recall when they came back to this slide, and you are not there to explain it. Think carefully about how you can give your points clear context and meaning.

I see a lot of '1 in 3', we reach 'x million' or '45% agreed...' What about the other 2 in 3, and is that x million important? Is that a significant number? Relative to what? And what about the 55% that didn't agree? These might be amazing stats, but without the audience seeing the context when they come back and read these in a few weeks' time, they might be left wondering.

If the 1 in 3 is more than anybody else, make that the point: 'reaching the **largest audience** with 1 in 3 coming to us'. Give pure numerical claims a reference point such as '**more than half** the available demographic consumes our content, with x million visiting each month', and explain why the audience should care when you give them just straight statistics or a piece of research: 'for the **first time ever** 45% agreed that ... '.

Don't leave it to chance and hope that your numbers speak for themselves and your audience will recall why this matters to them.

Make these points clear within your highlights and this will significantly improve your slide impact when you apply the Soundbites.

Step 3: Finding the slide Soundbites

First up, let's talk about what goes on a slide and why this matters.

The slides are there to support you in landing the narrative, getting the key pieces of information across and supporting your audience when they come to review or share your content. They can also help you present, but they should not be designed with only that purpose in mind. The primary job of the slides is to connect the audience to your content and to help them comprehend the ideas and solutions you are sharing, which may be brand new to them. They should break down complex concepts into simple nuggets of information and visuals rather than wordy, statistics-heavy charts and complex diagrams that few understand.

The slides and the presenter need to work together; you should add value to what is on display, not just read word for word and click on the next slide. Each slide should **enhance the point** you are making **and make it easy to understand**, which is the relationship a Strategic Storyteller is constantly looking to achieve.

Remember this important point: **you want to control the narrative, even when you are not there. What you draw attention to on the slide is the only way you can be sure this is the case**.

Armed with your narrative and your highlights, you are now ready to refine your slides and ensure these support you and your content by delivering the right Soundbites in the right places at the right time. **Soundbites are the nuggets of information your audience should not miss.** The goal is to have slides that are easy to understand and impossible to misinterpret. And these are not the same thing. When you bring together your narrative and apply Soundbites you won't just have a layout and slide navigation that aids in landing your message; you will also be precise in the point you want someone to take away and recall, leaving them without any doubt about what that could mean.

THE 1, 2, 3 OF SLIDE LAYOUT

	POWER UP	SUSTAIN	REFUEL
HERO SLIDE			
ESTABLISH			
EXPLAIN	The meal that gets you going	Fuel on the go	Nutrition for another day
NARRATIVE	Write the longer story that you want to share within each section away from slides. What would you share if we were chatting? What is the storyboard for this presentation?		
HIGHLIGHTS	Highlight the most important points that need to be landed within each section		

Apply the 1, 2, 3 of slide layouts

	First scan	Connected short cuts	Order of three
SOUNDBITES	The biggest and most prominent should be the most important.	The role of the picture, chart or graphic on a slide is to support the main point. It is a short cut to make the point stick.	Order matters up to three points; don't distract from these points with new content.

You now know your overall narrative, and you have your highlights to get across. The question you need to ask now as you look at every slide you have is this: how is this slide supporting this story within the overall narrative, and what is the main point I need the audience to take away from this slide?

A slide can carry three points, which should all be connected and related to each other; after this, you begin to dilute everything on the slide or confuse the audience, either as you present or when they come back to review your content to find what they need. This doesn't mean there are only three things on the slide; it means you can only expect to get across three pieces of new information, and to aid comprehension these things should all connect. You want to avoid adding information that may distract from these three pieces of information, and anything else on display needs to be so insignificant that if it is missed, it doesn't matter.

You then design your slide so you signal what is most important by making this the most prominent, the thing that catches the eye in that first scan, and that any image or visual cues support, and the two other points in clear view flow on from this.

There might be other details on the slide, but just know that after three points, these won't be recalled, so if they are important, give them their own slide.

Be very deliberate about this

What do you want the audience to see first, take away from this slide and be able to find later? That should be in the largest font and in the most prominent location, which for most slide layouts means the slide heading.

Then what supports this? This could be a callout of a key statistic from a chart; it might be an essential supporting point for your slide heading; it could be a piece of evidence, research or diagram that brings your explanation to life.

As I touched on earlier, ensure you make data points and statistics clear in terms of what you want the audience to take away, but also make it clear where that data point is if you are including a chart. Don't just insert data tables, charts and research findings. Call out, highlight or put a box around the specific part of that chart or table you want the audience to see and make it clear why you want them to see it. This will help you get to the point and not talk through every data point on the slide, and it will help them recall the key point.

Each slide should deliver something you don't want your audience to miss, and connect and flow as part of the overarching narrative.

Be very aware of overloading your slides with too many key pieces of information.

Be very aware of overloading your slides with too many key pieces of information, and of breaking the flow with information that isn't connected to the main point. Be clear, specific and simple in your explanations. There are no prizes for being arty when you are trying to move your audience through a story; avoid abstract points within your slides and keep asking yourself, is this the cleanest and most logical way to move them through this story, and this slide? How do each of the points flow and connect?

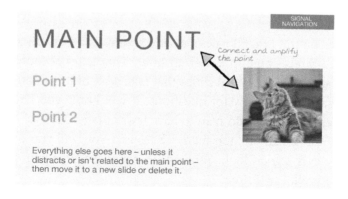

Don't waste the headings

I am a big fan of slide headings, but only when used as a critical piece of content to aid flow, navigation and recall, and clarify what a slide is about. They are one of the most underused and wasted parts of slide design. They should carry your most important point and not some random heading related to your process, such as 'Our approach' or 'The insight', or a cute phrase, such as 'Why we like this'. This is a waste of attention and isn't important.

Please don't waste the opportunity to make your point in the most prominent position; slide headings are not placeholders. They are a sales opportunity; sell your significant points.

HOW MANY SLIDES ARE TOO MANY SLIDES?

So now is a good time to talk about slide count. There are some good reasons to obsess about slide count, and times when more slides are better than fewer.

I work on the general rule of a slide a minute; a sixty-slide presentation will rarely come in under an hour. That takes account of slide dividers and more technical slides that take a bit of unpacking, and of course that doesn't allow for questions. If you know you have a one-hour meeting, you should plan to have fewer than 50 slides.

Slide count matters; too many slides and you will run over time, which is never a good look. You have to plan your slide count to work within your allocated time.

But here is the contradiction: always add slides when it aids the flow of the story. If a slide has grown to have more than three important points, create a new slide and split the points between them.

If slides are becoming text-heavy, split them into two.

If you have too much content creeping onto a slide – say, a supporting chart or diagram and it distracts from the main point – create a separate slide for the diagram and carry the heading across to connect the two.

You get the idea.

Keeping your audience following your story and being able to recall and find the slides they need is critical. **Slide count is not as important as clarity in your message.**

So while slide count is important, coming in on time with a presentation that makes no sense is not going to win you anything.

There are always places to trim the slide count. Developing a flowing narrative in the core navigation of the story should take precedence, and once that is in place you can cut from your set up, problem summary or 'about you' slides to get the overall count down if needed.

Not everything needs to be or should be a slide. What can you write, show, say, and not say?!

▶ Write headings that will tell the story.

▶ Leverage pictures and diagrams to make complex ideas easy to understand and support the headings.

▶ Show and say key points that emphasise how you give them what they want and solve for winter.

▶ Use your spoken narrative and notes to meet their unspoken needs.

▶ Don't say what can go into leave-behinds, handouts (whoever is attending from your team could send these over before the meeting or have printed for the table to save five minutes of introductions), appendices and follow-ups sections.

If you use the tools in this book, you can avoid being the most annoying type of Hopeful Presenter. They hope they can get through all their slides in the time they have; roughly a third of the way in they realise they can't, or they are given a prompt by someone in the audience that time is running out and could they *get to the point*! Then, rather than deciding what is most important and navigating to that, they just speed up. Continuing with the same linear flow, reading every point on every slide, just at twice the speed, with absolutely no chance of anyone remembering anything they have just had to sit through.

Don't be that person.

SOUNDBITES CHECK

As your slides come together and with your narrative and highlight list in hand, you want to keep a check on your story. Come out of slide view and put your presentation onto slide sorter view so you can see at least one whole section of the presentation on the screen.

Now, look across the slides like they are billboards and you are driving past them on the road, just getting a fleeting second or two to take in the content on display.

Ask yourself:

► What stands out?

► What headings and key points can you clearly see?

► How well does what you can see connect and flow as a logical story?

► Are all of your highlights visible?

If what you see isn't working, if the points aren't clear, if it is a bit clunky or if you are missing key highlights from your list, change it now. And by changing it, I mean adjusting the headings, making the font larger and making the points shorter and punchier so they stand out more.

You are not rewriting pages of content; by now, hopefully, your solution and the core of your content are solid. Your job here is to make it clear, easy to understand and easy to follow.

SOUNDS LIKE BORING SLIDES TO ME

Doesn't this take all creativity away from slide creation and make them all the same – very dull and boring, which surely would impact the audience's attention?

What this is not is a template for where on the slides things go, a fixed and rigid layout of the headline top left and sub-points two lines below in two-point smaller Arial.

You can still use the full canvas of the slide however you want. You can have images behind the text, text floating across images, you can have headlines in the middle or anywhere on the slide, just as long as you follow the principle: what you make look the most important is the most important.

You want to make it easy for the eye to follow the order. Logic is your friend. You can use creative placement and then add numbers at the start of each point to signal the order if it isn't obvious. And you want everything on the slide to support one clear point, not 12 – or, as I have seen in one case, 24 different points!

There is a lot of creative freedom available, and opportunities to make your mark and bring your brand personality and style into your slides and still land the Soundbites that deliver the narrative you need your audience to recall.

SOUNDBITES

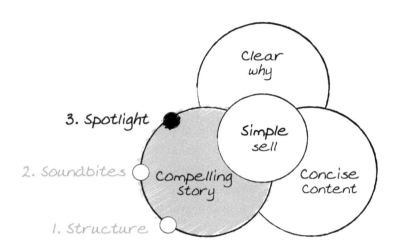

Avoiding regrettable and forgettable presentations.

'Can I have an hour of your time to come and talk about me and all the cool stuff we have and give you an update on what we have going on?'

Oh boy, do you love having the spotlight on you! How do I know? I see it every day in presentations. Hour-long slide festivals that are just about you and all the wonderful things you have done and want to do next, and not a slide in sight that I have any reason to care about.

I call these regrettable and forgettable presentations.

These are regrettable because we both wasted an hour, and forgettable because there is no connection between what you have and what I might want or need, and, therefore, nothing stored away to recall down the track.

Now that might sound a bit harsh, or it may be resonating a little too much. Either way, there is an approach to determine where the Spotlight is and resolve any imbalance before you present.

Even with all of the work you have done so far, you still want to do one final check of the overall balance of your content.

The goals are:

▶ to ensure the Spotlight isn't just on you for the whole hour

▶ to ensure the presentation isn't just about all the benefits they get without some supporting substance about how you do this and what makes you unique, special or able to do it.

In the final push to get slides finished, the pendulum can swing either way without you really noticing. So let's consider the issues at either end of the scale before looking at the very simple final check you should do.

As I have covered quite extensively throughout this book and for one final time here, when the Spotlight is on you for too long with content that is all about how great you are, how you came up with these amazing ideas, how big your market is and how many new products you have coming up this year, you run the risk of boring your audience. There is little to connect you, and this content can be easily forgotten.

In response to this, however, it is possible to go too far the other way: to make every slide or the majority of them about the benefit of working with you, the engagement, connections, sharing, drivers, impact, ROI, growth, improvement, transparency and click-through rate.

And about now, you might be thinking, *And what is wrong with that? Isn't that what you spent half a chapter telling us to do?* Sort of; the danger here is if you take this too far and, with that, your content comes across like a game of buzzword bingo, with the audience ticking off each catchy marketing phrase but left wondering how you do this, what your secret sauce is, and what they are actually buying or buying into.

And that is the importance of balance, which is achieved when you have *what and how in combination with why this matters.*

Consider the following image. Typically, most presentations lean to the left; that is, too much about you, playing in the rationale and expected space. What this means is the vast majority of the final adjustment is to ensure that the benefits to the audience and some more emotive elements are coming through in the slides.

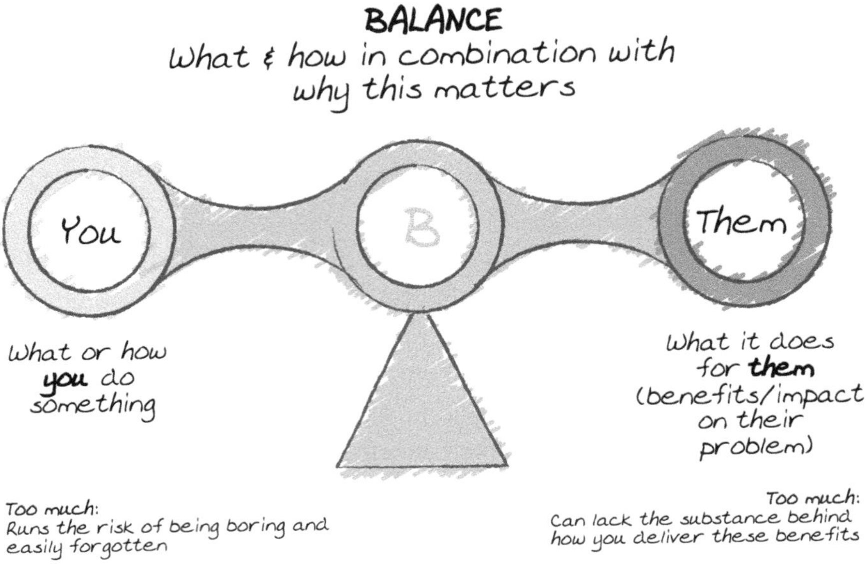

BALANCE
What & how in combination with why this matters

You   B   Them

What or how
you do
something

What it does
for **them**
(benefits/impact
on their
problem)

Too much:
Runs the risk of being boring and
easily forgotten

Too much:
Can lack the substance behind
how you deliver these benefits

RATING YOUR SLIDES

Rate every slide you have based on the Soundbite. When you look at the main point of that slide, is it:

▶ What or how **you** do something – tick ABOUT YOU.

▶ What it does for **them** (benefits/impact on their problem) – tick ABOUT THEM.

▶ Clearly demonstrates a **benefit** and **how** this is achieved – tick WHAT & WHY.

There is a template at the end of this chapter and you can download a copy at: www.davidfish.com.au/downloads/wp, but you can also do this on paper or a spreadsheet while looking at your slides in slide sorter view. Write the slide number and then ABOUT YOU, ABOUT THEM, WHAT & WHY next to each one.

The advantage of using the template and writing down your Soundbites is you can also check the flow and clarity of your narrative and see if your highlights are all still clear at the same time.

What are you looking for? The first obvious one is that all of the slides are not just about you; the Spotlight shining on just you for an hour and 60 glorious slides. The second check is that you don't take too long to reach content that is about them; you don't want to be halfway through your slides and still not have landed something that demonstrates some form of benefit to them, giving them a reason to care about your content. Ideally, you would get to this in the first few slides. And then across all of your slides you want to achieve a reasonable semblance of balance; that is, there are as many about them slides as there are about you slides, or the majority of your slides deliver the what and why. Finally, you want to see how the content flows between you and them. You don't want 30 slides about you and then 30 slides about them.

Then make changes to establish a better balance as required, as described in the following sections.

If there is too much about you

What can you change in slide headings or the main points on the slide to elevate the benefits and the impact of this content for the audience? Where can you more overtly show the change your work will deliver and how it is solving their problem? This is nearly always possible by making changes to the existing slides rather than creating new ones.

Apply the 'why should they care?' filter to your highlights.

A heading that says 'We are No. 1 in this demographic' is about you. Same slide content but a new heading that says 'The scale to help you grow' is now about them. Honestly, it is that simple, but if you take the time to do this throughout your slides, to tune the balance from 'all about you' to make more of the slide talk to them and their needs, it will change the entire feel and, more importantly, the way your presentation connects with your audience.

SPOTLIGHT

> **What can you change in slide headings or the main points on the slide to elevate the benefits and the impact of this content for the audience?**

If there is not enough about you

Either you have gone too far in making every point about a benefit, and this is masking how you deliver the work, or there just isn't enough about what you do. I'll be honest – this is a very rare challenge indeed!

In either case, you need to add in or perhaps dial up more of what you are doing to bring this into balance. This could be a slide or two after you have landed on what this does for them to highlight how you deliver this.

This is designed to be both a super simple and a very quick exercise, but it is one that can close that final gap and take you from good to great!

Side note: *Good to Great* is the title of an all-time classic leadership book by Jim Collins. It has absolutely nothing to do with presentations, but I still recommend everyone reads it.

SPOTLIGHT

Balance exercise

Soundbites – write the highlight of the slides as a list	Balance		
	About you (what)	What and why	About them (why)

SPOTLIGHT

Compelling Story conclusion

In this toolbox, you learned how to create a presentation designed to deliver your content through a compelling story with three new tools. You now know how to structure your presentation around a story arc specifically designed for selling ideas and ensuring that the most important parts of the story are the most prominent and visible within your content and slides. Research shows that recall of information is much improved when it is shared in a story. Your story needs to get the audience from point A to B as cleanly and logically as possible. Learning the art of storytelling will increase your confidence in your ability to deliver a compelling presentation.

Once you have the three-stage story arc worked out, it is time to enhance how you deliver content by getting down into the format of slides. Soundbites are all about how you take the content sections that live within your navigation and move from the high-level sections down into the narrative that will connect your key points, and then how this flows through to form a story within the slide itself. You want your audience to be able to easily recall the point you make on each slide as well as how you can help them find what they need in all of your content after you leave.

Too often I see hour-long slide festivals that are just about you and all the wonderful things you have done and want to do next, and not a slide in sight that I have any reason to care about. You must do one final check of the overall balance of your content, to ensure the Spotlight isn't just on you for the whole hour, and to also ensure the presentation isn't just about all the benefits they get without some supporting substance about how you do this and what makes you unique, special or able to do it.

You're now well placed and ready to take all the work you've done and condense it into its smallest but most potent form with Toolbox 4: Simple Sell.

TOOLBOX 4:
SIMPLE SELL

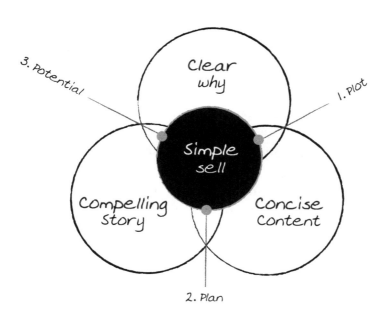

The ultimate presentation is a simple one.

Perhaps you've heard the quote, 'Simplicity is the ultimate sophistication' (often misattributed to Lenoardo da Vinci).

But getting to a simple story isn't simple. Simple is probably one of the hardest things you can do, but it is also the most rewarding and, when done well, incredibly powerful for communicating ideas and solutions to others. When you know your content in its simplest form, you are equipped to be able to share it with anyone. You can provide a high-level snapshot in 10 seconds to a CEO or sit down and expand on the details over a coffee with a subject matter expert. You are no longer paralysed by fear at the prospect of not having the full hour to present or not having your slides to remind you, and, critically, you can make it easier for others to hear your story and then share it.

This is what every Strategic Storyteller should aim to master.

SIMPLICITY IS THE ULTIMATE OUTCOME

To simplify something requires preparation, and as a result it is not the first step but the last. You need to know what you want to say, and have organised everything you know and need to support your points. You will have refined your long story to be the best version of a flowing, well-structured story with the key points now well understood and clearly defined.

It's the reason this is the last chapter. If I had put this first, you probably wouldn't have kept going because it would have seemed too hard. Everything you have been working through to this point has been preparing you and your content for this one last critical step to becoming a fully fledged Strategic Storyteller.

So having worked through the past three chapters to become Clear, Concise and Compelling, you're now well placed and ready to take all the work you've done and condense it into its simplest but most potent form:

- ▶ **Plot:** the story of change that you now know is possible.
- ▶ **Plan:** how you can deliver or will achieve this change.
- ▶ **Potential:** the benefit you bring (why we should work together).

You are going to take the Hero Slide from the Visualise Tool in the Concise Chapter and create a single page that doesn't just have an overview of your content; it now has your entire presentation. Every presentation can be presented on a page, and when you have simplified your story to the point you know the Plot, the Plan and the Potential, this will be a breeze.

More than just a one-pager

However, don't be fooled into thinking it is just a pretty overview, a nice summary of your work. This is an invaluable tool.

With this knowledge, you can articulate with great clarity what your presentation delivers for the audience and the value in what you bring, helping you set up meetings and answer corridor questions such as, 'Hey, should I come to that presentation next week?', or, 'What is that meeting about?' No more fluffing around the edges trying to think of a way to summarise what you want to present.

You will be comfortable being able to present your story at any moment in the quick CEO or sales director overview chat when they ask, 'What are you presenting this week?' In a lunch meeting, you can draw the main message of your presentation on a napkin and explain what the benefits of working with you are and, should the need arise, you can still get a room of people across your ideas without the need for all your slides.

And then, when you have those days when meetings start late, you have to finish early or you are just told you have half the time that was planned, you can navigate through your slides to land the narrative in whatever time you are given. No more panic as you will know exactly what slides matter most in the time you now have.

When you can simplify the sell in this way, the confidence you have in your content and your story will reach its peak. Your audience will clearly feel how connected you are to what you are sharing, and as a result you will make it much easier for them to connect with you, which is what every presenter needs – to have the audience engaged, connected and able to take your content forward to keep you in the game.

SIMPLE

> **The Strategic Storyteller is ready for anything.**

When 90 minutes became 15

The faces in the room wore different reactions.

On the Channel Nine side, delight at the idea of a shorter meeting and time back. *The meeting will soon be over*, they thought. On our side, shock and despair were evident in ashen faces, all of this work and just 15 minutes to land our idea.

We were presenting to a group of senior executives from Channel Nine, from the head of news programming to their head of audience research and the CEO of the broadcaster, at the time David Gyngell.

The meeting had come about from a long-standing relationship, and it had created a rare opportunity to flex our strategic muscle and show what we could do in a very significant partnership between two broadcasting powerhouses; there was a lot at stake for us all.

The 6 pm nightly news is a key timeslot for television ratings. This is not only a peak viewing time and so of great value to advertisers, but also an important timeslot because it can set up the success of the program that follows and the whole night's ratings as those audiences follow from one program to the next. Basically, this means the 6 pm nightly news is one of the most important in the programming schedule and one to win in the ratings war as these ratings convert to ad dollars.

Nine, which had a reputation for leading in this timeslot with a proud heritage of producing the best news, were locked in a fierce battle with Channel Seven, which had now been leading in Sydney for some time.

We believed we had some strategies that could help Nine win, we just needed an audience. So when we heard that the meeting had been confirmed, I assembled a team and we hunkered down.

Our strategies needed substance and ideas to bring them to life. Within a few weeks, we had mountains of content, way more than we needed and certainly more than would fit into a 60-minute presentation with 30 minutes for questions from what we knew would be a large audience of interested parties.

SIMPLE

Eventually, a very polished and meticulously rehearsed presentation emerged; it was completed with at least an hour to spare before the meeting, as nearly always seems to be the case!

The meeting was first thing in the morning, and so after another quick breakfast run-through confirming roles, handover points and possible questions, we were finally ready for the big performance.

The boardroom at Nine was full, and we were all seated when David arrived; his breakfast meeting had run over and, after the pleasantries, he announced he only had 15 minutes before his next meeting. Could we please summarise the main points for him, and then we could continue with his team if there was interest?

There may have been an audible gasp on our side, or I may have imagined that for dramatic effect, but in any event it was a very dramatic change of events.

All eyes turned to me. I was the strategic lead. I owned the deck and knew the content better than anyone. *Come on, Fishy, land the story*, was written across the faces of our team, which also included some very senior figures from our business. I took a moment to compose myself, as the team bought me some time. I flicked out of the slide show view to slide sorter and did a very quick shuffle.

One set-up slide, drop the other ten straight to the Hero Slide and the story navigation on a page, and a couple of supporting slides that brought the ideas to life, and then to the summary of why this would work for both parties and how we saw this moving forward.

It was a new 10-minute deck built in less than one minute, and it was delivered with five minutes to spare for questions.

As David stood up to leave precisely at the 15-minute mark, he said, 'This is good. I like it – let's get a team together and work through what this can look like.' That was all we needed; we had the green light to move forward, and that was most certainly a win.

Three months of detailed research and planning followed, and today more than 10 years on I can still see elements of that work in the nightly news and the partnerships that continue.

Had we tried to speed our way through the slides, had we tried to execute a live cut down, had we not taken the time to simplify the

SIMPLE

strategy and define our headline narrative and the core message we could present on a single slide and get clear on the benefits within our ideas, we would not have been able to present this story at the very highest level in a coherent way with such little time to adapt.

It was the simplification of our strategy that saved the day; without this, we would have confused the hell out of everyone and been left licking our wounds.

This might be an extreme version, but this experience is not a unique one. It happens a lot; you think you have an hour to present, and you end up in a walking meeting for 20 minutes because there are no meeting rooms.

And, certainly, when presenting to senior executives and boards, you should expect that the time you have will be cut short. They are time-poor, running from meeting to meeting, and want to get to the point and expect that you know what the point is. Learning to become a Strategic Storyteller will prepare you for this and many other situations when you need to land a winning presentation without the full presentation.

The Hopeful Presenter might be overheard saying, 'I hope I can explain why this matters when I get asked what this is all about.' Or, 'I hope I don't need to provide a summary slide, since I have no idea where to start.' Or, 'I hope we don't have to present in the café because I have no way of delivering this without all the slides and my notes.'

CREATING THE SIMPLE SELL

If you have applied the other nine tools or at least one or two from each chapter, you will be well prepared and ready to apply this last set as they take what you already have and condense it down to its most potent form, elevating just the essential elements to sell your idea in its simplest form.

SIMPLE

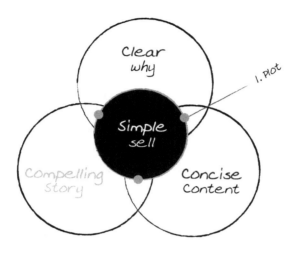

Your story of change.

The plot comes from the intersection of the work you have done to get clear on the change you see as being possible and working through your content to understand and refine this change in line with the content that makes it through to your Hero Slide. When you have defined the overarching sections of your presentation, you can go back and validate that this change is indeed possible and is delivered in your presentation content.

Once you've done that, you are now in a position to finalise the core plot line for this story, the story of change. This probably began as quite a functional statement, working from the problem to Winter up to the Better Place to define this change originally.

As an example, way back when I started developing this program, this was 'underconfident presenters who hope they can win' (A) to 'the confidence to present like a pro' (B). While this might be the start and end points of the change, it is boring; who wants to read a book or see a presentation about that?

The plot needs to be exciting and descriptive and create a sense of anticipation. 'I want to hear more,' and, 'I want to know how'; these are the reactions your plot needs to illicit. And to do that, you need to think a little more creatively about the change you are delivering, confident now in the knowledge you can deliver that change, having validated this by working through your content to get to your Hero Slide.

That is where Hopeful Presenter (A) to Strategic Storyteller (B) came from. This is the plot for this work in whatever form it is delivered; this book, the training, keynotes. That is my story of change, and it sounds a lot more exciting and interesting.

In the Concise chapter, when I was building the Hero Slide with all of my ingredients organised and optimised into the three sections of Power Up, Sustain and Refuel, I was working with this change:

Problem: High-performance sales teams, eating unhealthily.

Winter: A poor diet can lead to degraded mental capacity, and this can impact sales performance over time.

Better Place: Healthy habits that enhance performance.

Again, the idea of going from degraded mental capacity to enhanced performance with healthy habits was useful to establish the change at the outset of this work, but it isn't punchy or exciting.

Having done the work to build my Hero Slide and see how the three sections work to deliver on this change, with a little creative licence I can create a plot for this story that is a lot more interesting: From Nutritionally Vacant to Energised Sellers.

That sounds a lot more exciting; want to know how to become an Energised Seller?

The plot needs to be exciting and descriptive and create a sense of anticipation.

Your goal is to validate the change you started with by checking that your content delivers against this, and then make that change the most exciting, interesting, intriguing version you can to draw people into your story at this most elementary level – your story of change.

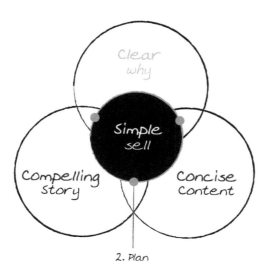

2. Plan

Shorthand for how.

With an exciting plot now in place, the next question your audience will have and want to seek validation of is how this change will be possible. *Do you really know how to do this?*

Preparing your Plan is about being ready for this and knowing how you describe the journey through your content at the highest level, with critical supporting points to add enough substance for whomever you are sharing this with.

The Plan comes from the intersection of your work on developing your Hero Slide and the Soundbites that call out your most critical points within the presentation itself.

The Hero Slide forms the core of this; however, it is now brought to life with a sprinkle of key points that add depth, validation and interest without getting down into the weeds of your content. To do this, simply read through all of the Soundbites you have created within your slides.

PLAN

Start a list for each section, and then decide what the main navigation point is and what secondary explainer or validating statement gives that section depth. Simply add these to a separate slide or even a simple Word document or notes page on your phone.

You can read these before you call to set up a meeting and before the meeting to remind you what you want to get across, in case you have to cut short a section or skip the slides but still want to explain your points. You can also use these in a follow-up email to summarise key points.

This is the Plan of how you get from the problem to the resolution at the simplest level with the most powerful points called out.

If I take my chapter on Getting Clear, this is what I have in my Plan, covering two levels of details (the majority of the time level one is enough):

Clear who this is for

▶ **Level 1: Who matters to you?**

Level 2:

- Your presentations can't be for everyone, ever.
- Who matters most to keep you in the game?
- The more your write for everyone, the less you connect with anyone.

▶ **Level 1: What matters to them?**

Level 2:

- When you know them, they know you are talking to them.
- The power of relevance and emotion.
- Moving from rational to emotional.

▶ **Level 1: The change you see as possible.**

Level 2:

- A presentation without a problem to solve is a presentation without a purpose.
- Problems are the gateway to your value.
- The greater the change, the greater the value.

PLAN

With these points to hand or – even better – committed to memory, I can overview my Plan at either the first level or drop into the second level and the points under each element if I need to, based on my audience's interest and needs. I can also quickly shortcut within my slides to hit the key points if I am pressed for time.

That is the point of the Plan – it is your shorthand for how you deliver the change through the points you have determined to be most important to demonstrate you've got this. It is not the full explanation of 'how'; it is just enough to instil confidence that you do know how.

PLAN

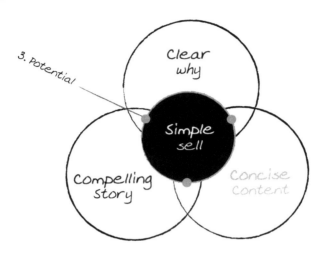

The change doesn't matter as much as the impact.

Throughout the work you have done to get here, there has been a lot of time and attention given to shifting your focus from what you do to thinking about why this matters to your audience and what is in this for them. This final tool is all about making the benefit you bring and why you should work together as simple and easy to articulate as possible.

The Potential lives in the intersection of the work you have done to ensure the Spotlight is on the benefits of your work and the problem that everything has been built around solving.

As you will have seen with the last two tools, you want to surface the most important points – in this case, the three or four major benefits that align with this problem – and make it clear why you should have a conversation, and why this presentation, the content, ideas and solution you have deserves to be seen.

You are not trying to list every benefit you have throughout your slides, although you might do that as a starting point. The goal is to end up with just those that really emphasise your impact, that truly define why this – *this* presentation, these slides that capture an idea or solution – matters to them.

When I look at the problem I am aiming to solve for my Hopeful Presenters, the highest-level benefits this work delivers is helping you become:

▶ Confident in the value of your message to your audience.

▶ Confident in how you bring your audience into your story.

▶ Confident in your ability to deliver a compelling presentation.

▶ Confident your audience can take your ideas forward and keep you in the game.

▶ Ultimately becoming a more confident presenter.

I know I have a stack more benefits throughout this book, but I also know that these are the ones I must ensure you know we are working towards above all else, and that is why they were in my introduction and have been reinforced countless times.

POTENTIAL

THIS BOOK ON A PAGE

Throughout this book, you have seen elements of the Simple Sell for this content; if I can get this whole book on one page, I am sure you can do the same for 60 slides.

Here is my simple sell on a page.

Plot
The story of change
that I know is possible

Hopeful
Presenters

Strategic
Storytellers

Plan
How this is achieved

Potential
The benefit of this; why we should
work together

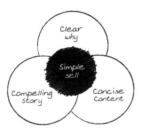

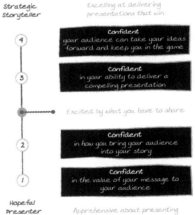

Clear about why this presentation
exists, who it is for and what
matters to them
Who Needs Change

Concise in the organisation and
visualisation of the content and
being able to turn every
presentation into a single page
Organise Optimise Visualise

Compelling through the story
that is told to bring the audience
into your content and connect
them emotionally to what you have
to offer
Structure Soundbites Spotlight

Simple is the ultimate goal for the
Strategic Storyteller
Plot Plan Potential

SIMPLE

Simple Sell conclusion

This final set of tools brings together everything you have worked on and enables you to refine your work one final time.

This is about you being armed with the highest-level summary that does justice to all your work while being as prepared as you can be for what might come next. Whether that is questions you get before the presentation or in your preparation to present, or the challenges that inevitably will raise their head as you present.

The confidence you get when you have applied these tools to Simplify your Sell will help you connect with your audience through not just your clarity of message but also how you deliver your content and help them to do the same after you leave. You will be extremely confident at this point that your audience can take your ideas forward and keep you in the game.

You now have what it takes to consistently create Winning Presentations.

> **The confidence you get when you have applied these tools to Simplify your Sell will help you connect with your audience.**

Part II: Conclusion

In part II, you have learned what moves a Hopeful Presenter forward to being a Strategic Storyteller. The four chapters in part II have covered the following:

- ▶ Be **Clear** about why this presentation exists, who it is for and what matters to them. Read this chapter to learn:
  - – How to define **Who** matters most to to you. Who is your audience.
  - – How to discover the audience's **Needs** and what matters to them.
  - – Why understanding the problem to be solved and the **Change** that you see as being possible is critical to every presentation.

- ▶ Be **Concise** in the organisation and visualisation of the content and being able to turn *every* presentation into a single page. Read this chapter to learn:
  - – How to **Organise** all of your content to increase its value and utility.
  - – How to **Optimise** the flow of information to make it easier to present and easier for your audience to follow.
  - – How to **Visualise** your entire presentation on a page.

- ▶ Be **Compelling** through the story that is told to bring the audience into your content and connect them emotionally to what you have to offer. Read this chapter to learn:
  - – How to **Structure** your presentations around a three-stage story arc designed specifically for this type of presentation that will bring the audience into your story and help you navigate them to your resolution.
  - – How to ensure that the **Soundbites** of your narrative land the key points you need your audience to remember.
  - – How to refine your content so that the **Spotlight** isn't just shining on you.

- Being **Simple** is the ultimate goal for a Strategic Storyteller who wants to be armed with the highest-level view of their work, prepared to share this with anyone in any situation while ensuring others are able to take their ideas forward, even if they never see a slide. Read this chapter to learn:
  - How to create an exciting and descriptive **Plot** that captures your entire story and creates a sense of anticipation.
  - How to summarise the **Plan** for how you get from the problem to the resolution at the simplest level with the most powerful points at the ready.
  - How to emphasise your impact, the **Potential** you bring that establishes why *this* presentation matters to them.

Grab the tools that make the greatest impact on your work and help you move forward the most, and give less time and attention to areas where you are already strong or have an approach that works for you.

This will work within whatever sales, strategy and creative process you already have, and can probably enhance quite a bit of it. You will be able to quickly work out how each tool slots into your existing ways of working, and they are cleverly designed to work incredibly well together. The real-world application of my work has always been key to what I do. This book is written to be by your side whenever you need it; it is not a read once, be inspired and move on kind of book. Apply the tools as you work through the many phases of developing your presentation and, particularly when you become practised at their application, you will wonder how you ever worked without them.

You will now have a narrative that guides you and will keep your audience following along with slides that tell your story as well as you do, giving you room to breathe and let your personality shine through as you bring these slides to life, no longer worried about missing a key point or stumbling over a random slide that appears out of nowhere.

WRAP UP

WHAT WE HAVE COVERED

What I believe and what I know to be true not just from writing this book but from what I see in the training, workshops and coaching I have delivered over the years is that – after reading this book – you will no longer be a Hopeful Presenter; that was only a moment in time because everyone has the capacity to become a Strategic Storyteller, and you are now equipped with the tools you need to create a lasting change for you. A change in how you think about your audience and approach your presentations. You can now create a platform that elevates both your content and your confidence.

You are ready to walk into a room, shoulders back, head held high, ready to take your audience on a journey through your content and guide them to the better place you know is possible. You are no longer apprehensive; oh no, you are excited by this change and by how your story flows from the wintery place you know your audience could end up in without you.

Presenting is now a joy because your audience is clearly engaged, by you and your content, following along, leaning in and eager to hear what's next. You are in control and clear on how to guide your audience to that positive and conclusive resolution that leaves them with no doubt about the value you deliver for them. It's hard not to smile as you hand over a presentation that you know not only gives them what they want and what they need, but also is set up to help them with whatever they need to do next, clearly solves a problem and will be both easy and enjoyable to present to others.

How does that feel?

All of that is what it feels like when hope is behind you, and now what lies ahead is the opportunity to continue to grow and develop your inner Strategic Storytelling skills.

> **Presenting is now a joy as your audience is clearly engaged, by you and your content, following along, leaning in and eager to hear what's next.**

You have graduated, and now the real-world application begins. Now it is time to make these tools work for you, your environment and with your ways of working, giving you the biggest advantage in helping with your greatest challenges.

The four toolboxes are structured around the flow of a presentation – I suggest you now reorder these into your personal power list, ranking them from 1, which is the most impactful for you, to 12, the least relevant for you. Mark the pages, use sticky notes or fold the corners so you can easily find the relevant sections for your power tools.

Then think about:

▶ How can you apply your top tools right now, literally *now*? Put the book to the side, open a presentation you are working on and apply the tools at this moment.

▶ Then, for the tools that are going to make the biggest difference for you, the ones you need to bring into your workflow, maybe you need to change the way you work or practise a new way based on what you have learnt; think about the smallest and simplest change you can make.

James Clear's excellent book *Atomic Habits* is, as the title suggests, about how we can change and form new habits that don't require great thought or effort; they become atomic. At the heart of this change is to make things as simple as possible.

Clear argues that small, daily habits have a compounding effect over time and lead to significant results. He advocates for focusing on incremental progress and continuous improvement rather than seeking overnight success. He advises making habits obvious, attractive, easy and satisfying.

So to bring these tools into your daily life, how can you break down what you need to do into the smallest possible change, what will make this easy for you to do, what can you do every day, and then, finally, how can you seek to measure or validate the change to make this as satisfying as possible?

Like all training, it is when we practise and when we apply things on our own, play with how things work when no-one is watching over us and begin to make them work for us that the real learning begins, and we adapt to find what really works on an individual basis.

These tools are now yours to use to support your journey to continue to leverage and apply them to make you a confident and engaging Strategic Storyteller who consistently delivers Winning Presentations.

12 tools that work independently and together

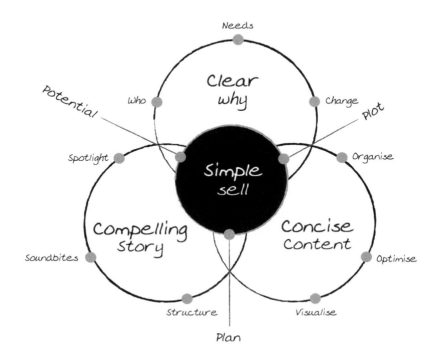

You can choose to use just one or all 12, taking advantage of how they work as a collection that builds through the presentation development process, with each adding greater depth and control for you.

The templates used in this book can be downloaded here:

www.davidfish.com.au/downloads/wp

If you would like to share your journey, learnings and success stories or to connect and stay up to date with my other training and coaching programs, you can contact me at:

fish@davidfish.com.au

You are a Strategic Storyteller, and the world needs more of you to be part of the movement to stop great ideas from getting lost in average presentations.

Fishy

Ingram Content Group UK Ltd.
Milton Keynes UK
UKHW021952020723
424437UK00006B/27